BREAKPOINT

The Changing Marketplace for Higher Education

JON McGEE

Johns Hopkins University Press
Baltimore

© 2015 Johns Hopkins University Press
All rights reserved. Published 2015
Printed in the United States of America on acid-free paper

2 4 6 8 9 7 5 3

Johns Hopkins University Press
2715 North Charles Street
Baltimore, Maryland 21218-4363
www.press.jhu.edu

Library of Congress Cataloging-in-Publication Data
McGee, Jon, 1962–
Breakpoint : the changing marketplace for higher education / Jon McGee.
pages cm
Includes bibliographical references and index.
ISBN 978-1-4214-1820-9 (paperback : acid-free paper) — ISBN 978-1-4214-1821-6
(electronic) — ISBN 1-4214-1820-7 (paperback : acid-free paper) — ISBN 1-4214-1821-5
(electronic)   1. Universities and colleges—United States—Administration.
2. Universities and colleges—United States—Planning.   3. Education, Higher—
Aims and objectives—United States.   4. Education—Demographic aspects—
United States.   5. Education, Higher—Economic aspects—United States.   I. Title.
LB2341.M364 2015
378.1'010973—dc23   2015006240

A catalog record for this book is available from the British Library.

*Special discounts are available for bulk purchases of this book. For more
information, please contact Special Sales at 410-516-6936 or
specialsales@press.jhu.edu.*

Johns Hopkins University Press uses environmentally friendly book
materials, including recycled text paper that is composed of at least 30 percent
post-consumer waste, whenever possible.

Breakpoint

For my Mother and Father,
who made college possible

Brayk • poynt *n.*

1. A point of disruption or discontinuity.

2. A point at which change must be made.

CONTENTS

Preface   *ix*

1 A Liminal Moment   1

2 A Brief History of [Contemporary] Time   8

3 Demographic Disruption   22

4 Economic Disruption   42

5 Cultural Disruption   64

6 No Line on the Horizon   83

7 Toward a New Marketplace   100

8 Reimagine the Future: Think. Different.   107

9 Breakpoint   142

Acknowledgments   *145*
Notes   *149*
Index   *165*

I have spent more than two decades studying demographic and economic trends in higher education, the past fourteen years as a cabinet officer at two liberal arts colleges. Like anyone reading this book, I have found that my perspective has been shaped by my own experience of the world. Where you stand really does depend on where you sit.

The College of Saint Benedict and Saint John's University are private, Catholic, liberal arts colleges located in Minnesota. Each institution is well reputed by any number of popular measures. Each enrolls between 1,800 and 2,000 traditional-age undergraduate students, most of them from the Upper Midwest. Neither college is highly endowed. Both are tuition dependent. All of those characteristics influence and frame not only our sense of self but also the choices we make. Every higher education institution could put together its own list of characteristics that shape who it is and how it thinks and operates. So, as you begin to read, I encourage you to keep in mind who you are and what shapes your worldview.

My personal history and experience also shape this story. Both of my parents were the first in their families to go to college. My mother was the only child of Italian immigrants who fiercely believed in the value of education for their daughter. My father was a beneficiary of the GI Bill and the only one in his family to earn a four-year college degree. A generation later, my parents sent my three brothers and me off to college, three of us to private colleges and one to a public university, all of them in Minnesota. We were not wealthy but were each able to attend the college of our choice because of the financial sacrifices made by our parents and because of the generous financial aid we received (and needed). From start to finish, the four of us attended college between fall 1980 and spring 1989. Over that nine-year span, my parents faced a total pre–financial aid cost of attendance of approximately $100,000.

Fast forward one generation. Like my parents, I too am the parent of four children. In fall 2015, the first of our kids will head off to college, the beginning of a postsecondary parade that will not end until 2028. If my children choose to enroll in the same colleges that my brothers and I selected a generation earlier, my wife and I will face pre–financial aid college costs that are between eight and nine times higher than the costs my parents faced to attend the very same schools, a gulpworthy, stomach-churning total by any definition. I nearly sent my wife over the edge recently when I casually announced (without warning) that we would need up to $1.1 million over the next fifteen years to finance the remaining years of our four children's elementary, secondary, and college education. The best answer I could muster to the exasperated "Why did you tell me that?!" question she rightly tossed back at me was, "I thought you should know." That kind of conversation, with all of its attendant hope and worry, happens around kitchen tables across the country. How will we pay for our children's college education? Make no mistake, economic factors are the central force influencing and reshaping higher education today.

Over many years, I've had the opportunity to work with many different colleges and types of colleges. Three career lessons stand out for me.

First, it's important to gather as much intelligence as possible about your place in the market. The stakes are too high for guessing, wishing, and hoping. Data collection and a commitment to insight and discovery are key. Edna Mode, the wonderfully eccentric fashion designer featured in the Disney/Pixar movie, *The Incredibles,* said simply as she was preparing the superhero protagonists for action, "Luck favors the prepared." Luck may not be the right sentiment, but success absolutely favors the prepared.

Second, though demographic and economic forces impact institutions in different ways, all institutions, the greatest and the least, are either directly or indirectly subject to the external pressures of the marketplace. Clare Cotton, the long-serving former president of the Association of Independent Colleges and Universities of Massachusetts was fond of saying that all colleges and universities ultimately are linked in a chain, each one ten up and ten down. I agree with him, though I would add a sideways dimension for our most immediate competitors. No institution is independent of the big changes occurring around it; all institutions are subject to the wave-like ripples of marketplace trends.

Finally, and perhaps most importantly, leadership matters—a lot. Board leadership, presidential leadership, staff leadership, and faculty leadership. Complex choices are not easy. They require consideration and conversation. They demand an assessment of both risk and values. The business of navigating in turbulent and deep waters is not for the faint of heart. All choices, even the choice to do nothing, have consequences.

I have framed much of my argument in the pages that follow using data to describe a number of big trends influencing higher education today. Big trends typically play out over large populations and over long periods of time. Averages and medians, and the occasional quartile or decile, become the currency of conversation, the markers by which we watch and evaluate change. The national dialogue about higher education today—often limited in scope and overly simplistic—typically feeds off of grand averages drawn from massed information about students, families, and colleges. Average student borrowing has risen to x, the average cost of college has risen to y, the average family income of college students is n. And so on.

There is a place in the analytic and reflective world for grand averages. They provide a useful mnemonic for identifying, understanding, and assessing change. And they provide an important antidote to the temptation and tyranny of anecdote—the risk of using one story to simplify or broadly describe complex issues and choices. But grand averages and massed data also put us at risk of depersonalizing what is ultimately a very personal experience: the business of choosing a college, the business of teaching and learning, and the business of picking a life path that is exciting and fulfilling. Big data rarely capture the emotion, or the intensity of emotion, that underlies both the college choice and the college experience.

The trick is to humanize deep knowledge about broad trends, leaving neither grand averages nor anecdote to stand alone as truth. Higher education ultimately is about individual people, not widgets. While averages and production functions provide useful insights to guide decision making (for students, families, and colleges alike), at the end of the day colleges need a far more granular understanding of themselves—their motivations, their operations, and their aspirations—before they act.

While much of the narrative in this book focuses on the large demographic, macroeconomic, and cultural forces shaping undergraduate enrollment at colleges and universities today, my principal aim is to encourage college and university leaders—trustees, presidents, administrators, and faculty—to use data as a launching point for understanding more about themselves and their particular place in the higher education world. While grand trends and averages may be interesting, even fascinating, our primary obligation is to better understand ourselves and our own markets, our own challenges, and our own opportunities to provide the best opportunities we can for the students we serve. Effective decision making requires a strong commitment to understanding the broad market forces at play around us as well as a strong understanding of self.

The decisions we make as higher education leaders have direct consequences for current students and generations of students to come. The collegiate experience remains principally characterized by an interpersonal intellectual and developmental exchange, one that has defied assembly-line mass production for hundreds of years. In economic parlance, each student remains her or his own unique production function, providing a mix of both inputs and outcomes. The interaction of college and student often is messy and unpredictable, but it is precisely that which makes it worthy, important, and sometimes even magical. The experiences we deliver may best be described as a trust, a one-at-a-time investment in future possibilities. College is the bridge between potential and opportunity.

The chapters that follow define the issues and imperatives of a demanding new marketplace for higher education. Chapter one provides a framework for understanding the social and economic change unfolding around us. Chapter two presents the extraordinary market conditions that shaped the two decades prior to the Great Recession as well as the immediate effects of the historic downturn. Chapters three through five describe the demographic, economic, and cultural forces of disruption that converged in the recession's wake to fundamentally alter the landscape in which colleges and universities operate today. Chapter six suggests how I think those converging trends will shape and influence our marketplace practice. Chapter seven and chapter eight focus on comparative advantage and provide a framework for addressing the disruptive forces playing out around us. In chapter nine, I provide some concluding remarks about our need to figure all of this out to create sustainable futures for ourselves and for our students.

I present these ideas not as a disinterested scholar of higher education nor as an education outsider looking in from the outside but rather as a college practitioner and leader who sits at a real table and contributes to real decisions on a daily and weekly basis. I also write from the vantage point of a soon-to-be college dad. The trends and issues I have outlined matter a great deal to our institutions. They also matter a great deal to prospective students and their families. We need to wrap our minds around them, define their particular consequences, and then act in a determined way to address them.

By way of fair warning at the outset, I do not offer either specific or universally applicable solutions to the challenging trends I describe. I don't believe that ready-made over-the-counter prescriptions exist, nor should they exist. It is more important, and more appropriate, that individual institutions understand how their particular part of the world is changing and then construct solutions appropriate to their circumstances, hopes, and dreams that allow them to address the challenges that change brings. The solutions must always be defined by our unique institutional context. As such, they are best gleaned from a well-constructed process that asks the right questions.

I have tried to provide a particular perspective on the forces of change operating on American higher education today. My ultimate purpose, however, is not simply to provide a descriptive assessment of a changing marketplace. Rather, it is to assist college and university leaders—and anyone committed to the future of higher education—to better understand themselves, their world, and their choices. No one person has all the answers, but working together to understand and take on the important issues of the day, we can make a big difference for our future and the futures of our students.

Breakpoint

CHAPTER ONE

A Liminal Moment

It was the best of times, it was the worst of times, it was the age of wisdom, it was the age of foolishness, it was the epoch of belief, it was the epoch of incredulity, it was the season of Light, it was the season of Darkness, it was the spring of hope, it was the winter of despair, we had everything before us, we had nothing before us, we were all going direct to Heaven, we were all going direct the other way.

—Charles Dickens, *A Tale of Two Cities*

A century and a half after it was written, Charles Dickens's opening passage in his classic prelude to the French Revolution offers a remarkably prescient description of the environment for American higher education today. It is clear that colleges and universities now live in the midst of a period of great change—a time that will challenge both their operating beliefs and their beliefs about operations.

Transitional points in history often result from the confluence of multiple seemingly unrelated events. While in retrospect the signals of change and their impact may appear clear, our real-time experience of change often is murkier and less certain. History does not usually come neatly wrapped in a bow as it unfolds. The transition from one historic period to the next—a liminal moment—typically is jarring as we become unmoored from the security of current context and practice and move to a future that appears less certain and less secure. Adaptation, innovation, and leadership become premium values during transitional periods.

Disrupted by long-predicted demographic shifts, jarring economic change, and changing cultural values about college, higher education today finds itself in its own liminal moment. The Great Recession of 2008 seamlessly morphed into an agonizingly slow and lengthy economic recovery. At the same time, long-predicted demographic changes in the characteristics of the traditional-age college population in the US have begun to take full effect. The combined effect of those two forces of change in turn have reshaped the way people think about the value of a college education.

Assumptions colleges and universities may have held as truths about their students, their families, and themselves have been continuously and uncomfortably challenged in recent years. What we surely hoped or expected to be temporary following the historic economic downturn has instead resulted in something more lasting. I do not believe we are simply biding our time in a temporary interruption of an historic trajectory. Instead, long-running economic, demographic, and cultural trajectories have taken new courses. The new pathways have produced a continuing disruption as families as well as colleges and universities have struggled to adapt to new and changing market conditions. The signature characteristic of the market's new trajectory, for colleges and families alike, is insecurity.

American higher education has entered a new world of increasingly complicated issues and challenging choices. We will continue to face more uncertainty than we had become accustomed to in the decade prior to 2008, when the Great Recession converged with long-brewing demographic change to fundamentally alter the postsecondary marketplace. Colleges and universities of all types will be challenged in remarkably complex ways to find new approaches to align their mission, market, and management practices with their aspirations. Nothing will be left untouched. The ways we approach prospective students, our pedagogical practice, curricular content and delivery, management structures—all will be subject to the pressure of change. The choices we consider will force assessment of both efficiency and effectiveness, and new ways to achieve both.

Conversations about issues influencing higher education most often are framed around questions of what we know. But if we begin and end only with what we already know, we won't go far. The more important question is, "How are you preparing for what you don't know?" We can take steps to prepare for what we know, but what we don't know or don't anticipate often places our organizations and operations at the greatest risk.[1] Planning models, which by necessity most often rely on the linear extension of current facts and circumstances, rarely provide us with the tools needed to accommodate unanticipated events or dramatic changes in direction.

Perhaps most importantly, we will be challenged to listen as never before: listen to our students and their families, listen to the signals of the marketplace, and listen to the values that formed and continue to drive our institutions. Opportunities and rewards will always exist, but they increasingly will be the product of creative thinking and thoughtful planning, not good fortune. Those who choose simply to roll the dice will learn quickly and painfully where their luck runs out.

The New Landscape for Higher Education

The landscape for higher education today can be framed around five key ideas and their attendant questions:

1. *Accessibility.* Who will have access to what kind of college experience? Will our institutions increasingly become places of destiny for the privileged or places of opportunity for the vast majority who are not privileged? These questions require an assessment of demography, institutional and family economics, market position, and public policy. We are nearing the bottom of a long-predicted, though shallow, decline in the number of high school graduates that began in 2010. The decline will be difficult for institutions accustomed to years of market growth. But the changing raw numeric totals mask a more compelling change: the characteristics of the traditional college-age population are rapidly changing in ways that suggest more, not less, difficulty with college access and opportunity. Most institutions will need to adapt to both the changing size and characteristics of the new market.

2. *Affordability.* How will students and their families pay for college? Without doubt, the cost of college has become the central challenge facing colleges and universities everywhere today. As the pre–financial aid price of college has increased at nearly all institutions at rates much faster than either consumer inflation or family income, angst about affordability has climbed sharply. Pricing and financial aid strategy most often seek to simultaneously maximize access and revenue, but that ground has become increasingly difficult to hold for many institutions. Moreover, the symbolism of the sticker price of attendance (the price before receipt of scholarship and grant aid) has become much more complicated. What does it mean if few students do or can actually pay the posted price of attendance? There ultimately are two sides

of the affordability equation colleges and universities must address: who can afford us and whom can we afford? Institutions must wrestle with both questions simultaneously, and the product must yield an equilibrium for long-term sustainability. The balancing act has become significantly more complex after more than five years of trying economic times.

3. *Accountability.* What kinds of outcomes ought students, parents, and society expect of higher education? What promises do we make to our students and how well do we deliver on those promises? Higher education collectively has struggled with how to answer those questions in understandable, persuasive, and compelling ways. That so many people enroll in college today demonstrates the extraordinary allure and promise of American higher education. That colleges and universities have been much less successful getting students to the finish line reveals an extraordinary weakness. Many are called, far fewer earn degrees. Four-year completion rates among new entering students at four-year colleges and universities in America average less than 40 percent, and have for more than a decade.[2] Our too frequent inability to muster convincing responses to accountability and value questions has resulted in an enormous amount of skepticism about both our motives and our operations, and has provided fuel to the rising tide of federal and state regulation all colleges and universities now face. We cannot understand the pressure on affordability independent of demands for accountability. In homes, in the halls of government, and in philanthropic circles, we face a singular central question: is this an investment worth making?

4. *Sustainability.* Can colleges generate the resources they require to continuously improve their academic and developmental quality and still remain accessible to students of all means? Unfortunately, those twin objectives very often compete with each other, particularly at less wealthy institutions—who comprise the vast majority of all colleges and universities in the United States—forcing a trade-off of one for the other. As importantly, questions about quality and accessibility get to the heart of revenue and expense realities. Colleges must assess both their *real* (not imagined or wished for) revenue opportunity and their *real* expense values and imperatives in the context of their *real* market position. Uncomfortable as these choices may be, most institutions will be forced to address them in some way. The marketplace will answer

for us if we choose not to answer them for ourselves. Equilibrium will again be the driving principle. The moment an institution is no longer willing to adjust its operations to meet its aspirations, its aspirations must change.

5. *Differentiation*. How will colleges distinguish themselves and their value in the face of increasing commoditization? College has in many ways become a transactional good rather than a transformational good, a necessary experience to improve the chances of success and security in a new economy. Unfortunately, the images and messages most colleges and universities send to the marketplace make it difficult for families to meaningfully tell them apart—which fuels the rush to commoditization. Colleges and universities of all types too often try to describe or distinguish themselves using the same limited set of images and adjectives, which results in a homogenized presentation that describes all institutions as friendly, caring learning communities dedicated to academic excellence and the development of the whole person. Images of smiling faces, lush grounds and ivy, overlaid with indistinguishable taglines and similar turns of marketing phrase, litter the mailboxes of prospective students everywhere. Me-too marketing is a perilous strategy in a commodity-driven marketplace.

These five issues present a particularly significant set of challenges to higher education leaders today because they operate both independently and interdependently. As stand-alone issues, none is easily resolved by the application of a few palliatives. Collectively, they form an even more difficult context in which colleges and universities must make their enrollment decisions, programming decisions, pricing decisions, and budget decisions.

A Language for Understanding Market Choices

Though this is not a comfortable subject to broach on campus, where a sense of history and traditional notions of collegiality often prevail, colleges and universities today must be understood for what they are: large-scale business enterprises. Institutions often enroll thousands of students, employ hundreds and sometimes thousands of staff and faculty, and provide an array of services that equal or exceed those available in small and even medium-sized cities. The days of tweedy mom-and-pop store management, characterized by informal structures and casual decision making, long ago passed.

Scale and complexity are not synonymous with soullessness, however. High-functioning institutions remain deeply committed to their mission and founding purposes, which almost always seek to advance a common good and serve a broad public purpose. However, the scale and complexity of operation at most colleges and universities today demands much greater emphasis on decision-making leadership skills and has caused (or should have caused) institutions to think more carefully about markets and market influences.

Ready, fire, aim is not a good market strategy. Of course, neither is willful ignorance. The kinds of students we enroll have changed. Their needs, expectations, and demands have changed. Where we seek students has changed, as has how we seek them. Public expectations of what we do and how we do it have changed. The stakes associated with our choices have risen as the needs and demands of the marketplace have changed. Few colleges and universities are masters of their own destiny. An inability or unwillingness to grasp or address the key trends at work around us can have disastrous consequences. Markets, and changes occurring within them, matter.

Each of the five issues framing the higher education landscape can be stitched together to form a set of triangles that encapsulate the most signifi-

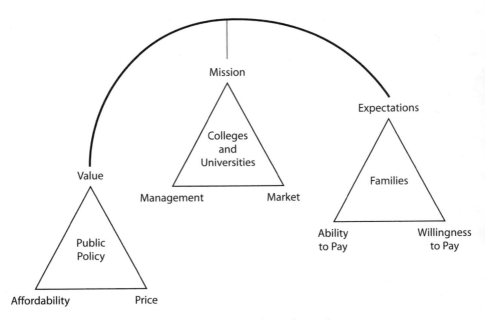

Seeking Equilibrium: Key Financial and Market Relationships

cant financial and market relationships at work today in higher education. From the vantage point of the broad market, three issues dominate the public policy discussion about higher education: price, affordability, and value. How much does college cost? How will people pay for it? What is the experience worth? From the vantage point of individual institutions, three similar issues drive decision making: mission, market, and management. What are we trying to achieve educationally? Who does and should attend my institution? How will we deliver our programs and experiences to our students? Finally, from the vantage point of students and families, three issues drive the way they prepare for and think about their college decision: ability to pay, willingness to pay, and expectations of the college experience. What resources do I have to pay for college? How willing am I to part with those resources so that I can have this particular experience? What do I expect for myself or my son or daughter from the college experience?

The individual points of each triangle align. Together, each of the independent triangles and their points must exist in some kind of balance both within and between for the market to function effectively. Think of it as you would a Calder mobile. The relationships are important; they drive both perceptions and choices. As colleges seek to balance their own mission, market, and management objectives, they must think in two other directions: what does the broad public conversation demand and what are the needs and expectations of the students we seek to enroll?

CHAPTER TWO

A Brief History of [Contemporary] Time

"I could tell you my adventures—beginning from this morning," said Alice a little timidly: "but it's no use going back to yesterday, because I was a different person then."

—Lewis Carroll, *Alice's Adventures in Wonderland* (Bookbyte Digital Edition)

By nearly any measure, American higher education ranks among the great organizational and industrial success stories of the last one hundred years. In 1946, fewer than 10 percent of all 18- to 24-year-old Americans were enrolled in college.[1] By 2011, that figure had risen to 43 percent.[2] The number of degree-granting institutions in the United States has increased by more than 2.5 times since 1950, while the total number of students enrolled at all levels of postsecondary education has risen nearly tenfold.[3] Today, the nation's 4,700 colleges and universities enroll nearly 21 million students of all ages, types, and abilities.[4] If there is a program of study that can be imagined, it probably is offered somewhere. US higher education is characterized by a remarkable intellectual, technical, and professional smorgasbord of choices.

Colleges and universities everywhere have been in the business of selling, occasionally hyperselling, the virtues of postsecondary education for decades, clearly to great success. But the pitch and sale, seemingly so easy to make, has resulted in changing expectations of higher education. And increasingly those changing expectations are cause for great discomfort. With apologies to higher education historians, the perceptual transformation of higher education in the United States in the last century can be framed in four broad stages.

Prior to 1945, college by and large could be understood as a *luxury good*. Relatively few had earned a college degree and few had access to college (largely because most people then had not even finished high school). In 1940, only 4.6 percent of all Americans over age 25 had completed a bachelor's degree or higher.[5] A college education in those days could be considered a macroeconomic luxury, as well. Because the US economy was still primarily a manufacturing and agricultural economy more dependent on physical human capital than intellectual human capital, its success prior to 1945 did not yet depend on mass access to higher education.

Following the enactment of the Servicemen's Readjustment Act in 1944 (better known as the GI Bill) until the mid-1960s, access to college was extended as an *earned privilege*, principally for military veterans. Access to college expanded for others during this period—enrollment of young women nearly tripled, for example—but veterans led the way. The launch of the Russian Sputnik satellite in the mid-1950s added motivation to broaden access to higher education. The effects of the GI Bill and the rising sense of the value of widely available college education were immediate and significant. The proportion of 18- to 24-year-olds enrolled in college rose from 10 percent in 1950 to 15 percent in 1960 and to 21 percent by 1965.[6] By the mid-1960s, half of all recent high school graduates in the country were enrolled in a college somewhere.[7] As the postwar baby boom reached college age, the table was set for massive expansion of postsecondary educational opportunity, growth that would be fueled by changing demography, war, and changing social and economic expectations.

With the passage of the Higher Education Act in 1965 and continuing until about 1990, America experienced the *commoditization* of higher education. College became a mass-market good supported by changing public policy[8] and undergirded by a changing economy increasingly less reliant on physical capital and manufacturing and more dependent on intellectual capital and services. Coming-of-age baby boomers, born in the aftermath of World War II, took advantage of both. High school–to–college continuation rates increased from 50 percent in 1965 to 60 percent in 1990. In 1965, just 12 percent of all Americans aged 25 to 29 had completed four or more years of college. By 1990, that figure had risen to 23 percent.[9] Led by rapid growth in the number of two-year and four-year public institutions, the US higher education system expanded dramatically to meet rising demand during this period. The number of degree-granting institutions in the country rose from 2,004 in 1960 to 3,056 in 1980. Public colleges (particularly two-year colleges) made up 60 percent of that institutional growth.[10] From an enrollment standpoint, these were, perhaps, the truly golden years of higher education in the United States.

Though more and more people took advantage of higher education as a mass-market good after 1965, it surely remained at its roots a transformational good, a signature experience offering a gateway to a better life than was available to prior generations. In 1966, just 30 percent of all college freshmen indicated that their father had earned a college degree (a degree not yet required for economic sustenance). Only 20 percent said their mother had a college degree. By 1990, reflecting the rise of a more education-dependent economy, nearly half of all new college students reported that their fathers were college graduates and more than one-third said their mothers were college graduates (numbers that have continued to rise since then).[11] For most students who enrolled during this period, college was a new family experience, and one that could create decidedly different economic and social opportunities than those available to their parents.

During the waning years of the twentieth century, with the birth and boom of the Internet and the advent of a truly global and integrated world economy (which expanded opportunity but sounded the death knell for much of the traditional manufacturing economy in the United States), higher education became a different sort of good. No longer simply a nice-to-have experience, a college education became a *necessity good.* As the return and opportunity associated with a high school education declined, and as demand for a more highly educated labor force rose, postsecondary education—often meaning *any* education beyond high school (two-year or four-year, degree or certificate)—became an increasingly necessary experience for access to the middle class and the hope of economic self-sufficiency and sustainability. The educational bar had been raised. In fewer than fifty years, college displaced high school as the threshold test for economic independence and success.

While no experience offers a guaranteed economic return, a college education has proven durable in good times and bad. Even during the depths of the Great Recession, unemployment rates for four-year college graduates were less than half of the rates for those who did not go to college.[12] Those who had only a high school diploma or less shouldered most of the burden of job loss during the downturn. The wage premium associated with college—particularly college completion—remains extraordinary. In 2011, the Georgetown University Center on Education and the Workforce noted that "obtaining a postsecondary credential is almost always worth it, as evidenced by higher earnings over a lifetime. The higher the level of educational attainment, the higher the payoff. What's more, the gap is widening. In 2002, a Bachelor's degree-holder could expect to earn 75 percent more over a lifetime than someone with only a high school diploma. Today, that premium is 84 percent."[13]

The signals to prospective students and their families are clear. While they often have significant concerns about rising college costs, parents today overwhelmingly expect their children to go to college. In 2012, more than 90 percent of all parents with at least one child under age 18 indicated that they expected their children to attend college.[14]

So after decades of growth and mostly favorable supporting winds, where are we today? In 2011, 68 percent of all recent high school graduates in the United States were enrolled in a college.[15] Nearly one-third of all 25- to 29-year-old Americans have earned a bachelor's degree.[16] A victory for certain, though perhaps one that is somewhat pyrrhic. The current public conversation about higher education all too often suggests that college is less a transformational experience than a transactional experience. The dialogue clearly suggests that the primary value of college is economic, not social or developmental or cultural or intellectual. Go to college, get a credential, earn a living. A straight path. The evolutionary trajectory is important because people view a product, service, or experience differently when it becomes a necessity than when it is a luxury. The stakes associated with going to college are higher than ever for students—and consequently much higher for colleges and universities, too. College leaders, inclusive of trustees, administrators, and faculty, would do well to recognize the perceptual and economic transformation. It has, at a minimum, fueled anxiety and more fervent calls for accountability and regulation.

New providers, new ways of obtaining degrees, new degrees, calls for shorter times to degree all suggest a new reality that many traditional institutions find uncomfortable. James L. Heft, Alton Brooks Professor of Religion at the University of Southern California, summed it up quite elegantly: "The commercialization of American culture tends to reduce human activity to exchange; it restricts the idea of value to a single, narrow measure—that of economic power. A friend of mine describes the United States as an economy with a culture loosely attached. Commercialization affects everyone in the academy: administrators, faculty, and students."[17] Social frameworks drive perceptions, and perceptions often drive experience. From the vantage point of colleges and universities, they shape both our opportunity and our challenge,

Yesterday and Today

In "Ode on a Grecian Urn," John Keats wrote, "'Beauty is truth, truth beauty,—that is all Ye know on earth, and all ye need to know.'"[18] Beautiful poetry, lousy social science. For most of the 1990s and up to the beginning of the Great Recession in 2008, colleges and universities across the country operated in a period in which the economic and demographic stars were aligned. This remarkable period created and fueled the conditions for enrollment and financial success at most institutions. Institutional operating strategies and tactics, as well as their aspirations, typically were designed to take full advantage of those conditions. Unfortunately, as the good times unfolded and rolled onward, seemingly endlessly, we placed ourselves at risk of believing that those favorable conditions represented truth, rather than a fleeting moment of beauty. The call of *laissez les bons temps rouler* played like a siren's song.

Demographic trends (which are largely predictable) and economic cycles (which most often are not predictable) exert significant influence on decision making at colleges and universities, driving our sense of opportunity as well our feelings of anxiety. How and when they occur is important. Because they typically play out over a number of years, we often are tempted to believe that current market trends, positive or negative, are permanent—a temptation that can lead to dangerously short-sighted decision making. Just as one year does not indicate a trend, five years (or even ten or fifteen) do not signal permanence or entitlement.

Demographic Gold Rush

In the wake of the "baby bust" that followed the postwar baby boom, the number of high school graduates in the United States fell by nearly 22 percent between 1976 and 1994. While enrollment calamity could have resulted from the precipitous and mostly continuous decline in traditional-age students over that extended period, that was not the experience at most institutions. In spite of falling numbers of high school graduates (who up to that point had by and large constituted *the* market for higher education), colleges across the country maintained or increased their total enrollment in three broad ways: they turned their attention to older students, tapping new markets in both undergraduate and graduate education; they benefited from rising high school–to–college participation rates among the declining number of traditional-age students; and they dramatically increased their enrollment of female students.[19]

By 1994, the long drought in high school graduate numbers ended with the coming of age of the "baby boom echo"—the children of the baby boom generation. Though not evenly distributed across the country, the number of high school graduates in the United States rocketed upward, rising by 36 percent between 1993–94 and 2008–09. The growth in high school graduates fueled an echo boom in traditional-age college enrollment. Between fall 1994 and fall 2009, enrollment of 18- to 21-year-old college students at all degree-granting institutions nationally jumped by 51 percent—meaning that colleges and universities not only rode the demographic wave to enroll more students but also succeeded in enrolling a higher percentage of the growing traditional-age market. Viewed another way over a longer period of time, enrollment of 18- to 21-year-old college students rose by 18 percent from 1970 to 1980, by just 2 percent between 1980 and 1990, by 17 percent between 1990 and 2000, and by an astonishing 30 percent between 2000 and 2010.

In other words, colleges and universities acted on the demographic signals unfolding around them and benefited from (and contributed to) the changing social and economic signals which favored college-going, to substantially boost their enrollment. Total undergraduate enrollment at American colleges and universities rose from 12.3 million in fall 1994 to 17.6 million in fall 2009, a gain of 43 percent.[20] Bigger was possible, and for many institutions, bigger was both good and better. It often resulted in more resources, more services, and sometimes even more prestige. For fifteen years, colleges and universities in all regions of the country lived on the equivalent of a higher education gold rush.

Boom: Let the Good Times Roll

At the same time that they benefited from a rising demographic wave, colleges and universities also took advantage of US economic growth of virtually unprecedented duration and depth. The 1990s and much of the first decade of the new century witnessed enormous wealth creation—though it was clearly not distributed evenly across the population—and, for at least a part of the time, strong family income growth. The signs of economic growth were everywhere, some seemingly comfortable, others less so.

The Dow Jones Industrial Average, a bellwether of economic health and wealth in the United States, hurtled upward from just over 3,300 in January 1993 to nearly 13,300 in January 2008.[21] During the same time period, the Standard and Poor's 500 Index of large companies more than tripled[22] and the NASDAQ Composite Index increased by nearly four times (even after accounting for the dot-com bust in 2000).[23] Growth was in the air, and it was reflected in broad economic indicators. Gross Domestic Product (GDP) in the United States, the most comprehensive measure of the nation's total economic activity, and Personal Consumption Expenditures, the broadest measure of household consumption of goods and services, rose by 114 percent and 124 percent, respectively, between 1993 and 2008.[24] Even adjusted for inflation, those broad measures of output and consumption each rose by more than 50 percent. Good times, indeed.

Consumer inflation (as measured by the Consumer Price Index) rose at an average annual rate of just 2.7 percent between 1993 and 2008—a modest rate of change over a protracted period of time, particularly after the inflation horrors that defined the mid-1970s and early 1980s.[25] The relatively slow rate of change in consumer prices was important. As the economy grew at a rapid rate, people could at least *feel* like they had more money in their pockets from year to year, even if their incomes were not rising rapidly.

From 1982 to 1992, the annual unemployment rate in the United States averaged 7.1 percent. The annual average dropped below 6 percent only three times over that period—making it the worst ten-year run for employment opportunity in the United States since the end of World War II. After reaching 7.5 percent in 1992, the US unemployment rate began to drop sharply, reaching its nadir of 4 percent in 2000. Unemployment rose after 2000, but reached 6 percent only once during the next eight years.[26] The employment experience for college graduates was even better. Between 1993 and 2008, the average annual unemployment rate for college graduates (those with a bachelor's degree or higher) never surpassed 3.5 percent and was at or below 2 percent from October 1997 to February 2001—essentially a reflection of full employment for college graduates.[27] The employment payoff to college seemed clear, perhaps clearer than it ever had been.

There were four recessions in the United States between 1973 and 1990, two of which lasted longer than a year. By comparison, the years between 1990 and 2007 saw only one recession and two of the five longest periods of economic expansion since 1900.[28] The economic expansion that preceded the dot-com-driven contraction as the century turned began in 1991 and lasted for 120 months (previous trough to peak). The expansion that followed the end of the brief recession in 2001 would stretch to 73 months. In total over the fifteen-year period, the United States experienced nearly continuous economic growth, the longest combined stretch of growth in US history. Expansion seemed never-ending and trend lines pointed only upward.

National economic growth benefited state coffers as well, allowing for rising taxpayer investments in higher education. Though not evenly distributed across all states, state appropriations for higher education operations nearly doubled between 1993 and 2008 (a gain of 32% in inflation-adjusted dollars), rising from $39.4 billion to $77.5 billion.[29] Most of those resources were directed to support the operations of public two-year and four-year colleges and universities, but some also were allocated to state financial aid programs intended to enhance students' access to college. Though higher education was clearly a beneficiary of rising investment, its *share* of total state expenditures actually declined between 1993 and 2008, falling from 13 percent to 10 percent—a cautionary signal that would play out with decidedly different results after 2008.[30]

For at least a portion of the long period of economic expansion, families benefited from rising incomes, aided by the robust labor market that defined the first half of the fifteen-year period. Inflation-adjusted median income for families with children under age 18 rose by a remarkable 19 percent between 1993 and 2000. The incomes of families with children grew almost 50 percent faster than incomes of families without children during that seven-year stretch (20% versus 14%), a particularly good turn of fortune for colleges and universities seeking to enroll traditional-age students.[31] Family incomes rose faster from 1993 to 2000 than they had in the prior twenty years, making the period something of a welcome return to good old—or at least better—days. Unfortunately, the year 2000 would prove to be the zenith for median family income for the period of 1993 to 2008 (and in all of the years since 2008).

While incomes rose for only part of the period, family net worth increased consistently and significantly from the 1990s through the first years of the new century. Between 1992 and 2007, median inflation-adjusted family net worth jumped by 68 percent. Accumulated wealth (measured by net home value, stock, and other financial and nonfinancial assets) became a much more substantial part of families' economic wherewithal. By 2007, income accounted for just 39 percent of median family net worth, down from nearly

54 percent in 1992.[32] Two notable trends helped fuel the rise in family net worth. First, and most importantly, home values (measured by changing home prices) rose by nearly 150 percent between 1993 and their peak in 2006.[33] As the signature asset for most families, rising home values not only increased net worth but also vastly expanded families' access to capital. Homes were not only a place of residence but also a piggy bank for future spending. Though the gains in home value ultimately would not prove to be lasting, or even real, families were wealthier, at least on paper, and could and would make spending decisions based on that rising wealth. Also influencing the rise in net worth was the flight to equities as stock market values rose. The percentage of families with direct or indirect (e.g., mutual fund) stock holdings rose from 37 percent in 1992 to 53 percent in 2007. Largely reflecting the rise in stock values, the inflation-adjusted median value of family stock holdings among those who held stocks more than doubled over the same period.[34] As with rising home values, neither of those trends would last. However, during the golden years of growth, rising stock values contributed significantly to the economic well-being of many families, providing them with new (and for many, previously unimagined) spending opportunities.

As incomes and net worth rose, families gained extraordinary access to capital that could fuel their spending needs and wants. If growth defined the economic trend for the period, then spending and consumption defined the economic behavior. Rising income and net worth provided families with extraordinary access to the means to satisfy what, in retrospect, seemed like an insatiable demand to consume. Americans embarked on an epic buying binge, much of it financed by borrowing. Outstanding consumer credit in the United States, which includes most short-term and intermediate-term credit extended to individuals, nearly tripled between 1993 and 2008, rising from $866 billion to $2.6 trillion in fifteen years.[35] Consumer debt rose by 53 percent even after adjusting for inflation—a rate of increase far faster than the growth in income, but consistent with the apparent but ultimately transitory increases in real net worth. In 1993, personal consumption expenditures for goods and services made up 67 percent of total Gross Domestic Product in the United States (it had remained unchanged for most of the prior ten years). Fueled by debt-based spending, by 2008, consumption made up 70 percent of GDP.[36] The US economy succeeds or fails largely on the basis of what Americans buy and consume, and consumer borrowing helped fuel economic success during the golden years of growth. Families seemingly flush with resources or access to resources found satisfaction that never before seemed possible.

Taken altogether, the economic trends that shaped the period created extraordinary conditions for operating success at colleges and universities across the country. The market conditions that seemed to raise the economic boats of families and states did the same for colleges and universities. Strong financial markets created opportunities for robust increases in college investments and endowments. State government appropriations buoyed enrollment growth and allowed for qualitative improvements at public institutions and in student financial aid programs. Family incomes and net worth rose, as did their access to debt capital, providing more students with greater access to more higher education options and enhanced pricing power at many colleges and universities. Robust employment outcomes for college graduates helped fuel demand for college. Whether we understood it or not at the time, these were the good old days.

Bust: Nothing Lasts Forever

The period 1993 to 2008 provided colleges and universities across the country with remarkable opportunities to succeed. The demographic trends could have been (and should have been) anticipated. After all, young people are not born 18. We had an opportunity to prepare for and capture the population growth, and many institutions surely did so. Few likely would now admit it, but there surely were institutions that neither anticipated nor planned for the demographic change but benefited from it nonetheless. It is good to be in the right place at the right time, though it provides few lessons looking forward if we have no idea how we got there.

The economic trends, on the other hand, could not have been anticipated so easily. They were not the product of our decisions, yet we had much to gain from them. The rising tide of the 1990s presented us with two key opportunities: how could we capture the benefits of strong economic growth to the benefit of our students and their experience, and how could we position our institutions for the moment or period in which the growth trajectory changed, which we surely knew or should have known was inevitable? Those same questions work for both upward- and downward-sloping trend lines. Irrespective of the particular characteristics of the current moment, all leaders are called to keep their fingers on the pulse of change, meaning they need to be attentive to opportunity and challenge as it presents itself now and over the longer term.

Though it began well enough, 2008 would prove to be a decidedly more difficult year than any of the fifteen years that preceded it. A few dismal statistics summarize the speed, scale, and ferocity of the change in economic fortune. After peaking during the last week of April 2008, the Dow Jones Industrial Average plunged by nearly 33 percent by the end of the year (a slide that would not end until March 2009). More than a decade of growth was wiped out in a matter of months. The unemployment rate began the year at 5 percent and ended above 7 percent (on its way to a high of 10% in November 2009). Average home prices, which had begun to slide in 2006, fell by more than 14 percent from the first quarter of 2008 to the fourth quarter of the year. Gross Domestic Product, which peaked in April 2008, fell by 2.3 percent by the end of the year, thrusting the country into its deepest recession since the Great Depression. The financial collapse touched every part of the economy and every part of the country.

The tumultuous economic events that began in 2008 immediately rocked the sense of security and confidence on campus in a number of important ways. Colleges everywhere had to assess the impact of the economic collapse on their students and families and quickly craft a response to address their (now very real and immediate) financial needs. Financial aid expenditures had already been rapidly rising, and the recession would push them up even further at many institutions. College leaders—particularly those at institutions with large investment portfolios that had benefited significantly during the economic run-up—also had to sort out and address the damage to their balance sheets, often forced to consider or make painful budget reductions to address significant losses in operating income. Public institutions faced immediate, and in most cases extraordinary, losses of taxpayer resources as state budgets shifted from surpluses to steep deficits. While some of those losses could be made up by raising tuition, the loss of state appropriations most often resulted in deep cuts to academic and administrative services at public institutions.

Any sense of complacency we may have accumulated during the long period of relative comfort was quickly jolted and more often uncomfortably wiped away. Most importantly, the economic events and changes that began in 2008 signaled a significant inflection point in the marketplace for higher education, crystallizing a set of forces that will continue to influence and shape our mission, market, and management opportunities for years to come.

What Next?

Why spend so much time reflecting on the demographic and economic trends that prevailed from 1993 to 2008? Because all colleges and universities experience, manage, and lead in context. Context shapes our sense of confidence and security as well as our sense of doubt and insecurity. And the context in this remarkable and remarkably long period could be described in just one word: plenty. In a period of expansion, we could afford to think, plan, and invest expansively.

Looking back through the prism of reflection, it is important to acknowledge that fortune always plays some role in defining our success or failure. We can neither anticipate nor control all of the events and circumstances that shape our opportunities and challenges. On the other hand, to leave success or failure purely to chance clearly exposes us to great risk (and even peril), as well as the temptation of lazy decision making or even willful blindness to the future. We must acknowledge the coexistence of luck and planning. We need to plan as best we can to anticipate and understand the environment in which we operate. At the same time, though, we need to recognize that our success also is influenced by good fortune, for which we cannot claim all of the credit (the trap of hubris). Planning and luck each are important because together they help us get our arms around the very real issue of risk—how it is shaped by good planning but influenced by issues and events not anticipated or out of our control.

All decision makers continuously are faced with their own version of a gambler's dilemma. Even when we acknowledge imperfect information and incomplete knowledge, we still judge reward on the basis of what we might gain by virtue of taking a risk. At the same time, though, we must be cognizant of what we cannot afford to lose when the winds of fortune shift or do not blow kindly in our direction.

For better or for worse, both clever and not-so-clever institutions were positioned to thrive during this remarkable period of growth from 1993 to 2008. It seemed possible, perhaps even wise, to plan upward to the rising tide of a boom that seemed endless. Unfortunately, by the end of 2008, it was clear that the good times would not go on forever. The golden boom period ended with a resounding bust, and institutions of all types were left with a considerably more difficult challenge: how well would the strategies employed during good times work under different circumstances in much more difficult times?

Forces of Disruption

A crisis is a terrible thing to waste.

Those words surely were uttered or muttered thousands of times on campuses across the country as trustees and college leaders wrestled with the effects and aftershocks of the Great Recession in 2008. However, while the term "crisis" clearly applied to anyone who lost their jobs or their homes or their life savings, it most often overstated the real challenges facing most colleges. Difficult and uncomfortable choices? Absolutely. Threat to operational existence? Not typically.

The language of crisis is vastly overused and regularly misused in our contemporary lexicon, to the point where it too frequently has become a rhetorical sentiment rather than a description of an actual emergency. Organizations and cultural pundits alike often apply it in ways that limit their ability to distinguish the interesting from the important and the truly urgent. While crisis typically is invoked as a catalyst for action, it just as frequently leads to a sense of despair or, sometimes worse, knee-jerk reactions that are unwise and unhelpful. The language of crisis also sends a signal that cataclysmic change is the only true motivator for change: absent an extraordinary event we will continue down the paths we have already set for ourselves.

Crises usually are perceived and addressed as time-bounded events. We can date-stamp when they begin and end, and at their close we move on. Worse, as they unfold we often fall prey to the trap of addressing the symptoms of the crisis rather than its root causes, not looking for a structural cure but rather an elixir that makes us feel better—like cold and flu medicine. If we determine that the effects of a popularly described crisis have missed us, then all the better. We were either brilliantly positioned in advance or simply in the right place at the right time. Either way, the storm passed and we suffered no damage.

The Great Recession and its lengthy aftermath demanded our full attention. Its immediate effects on our students and families, as well as our institutional operations, were inescapable and undeniable—and sometimes quite significant. But as it was a time-bounded crisis, if all we paid attention to was the beginning and end of the downturn, we would have missed the broader and more significant trends converging at the same time that continue to challenge us in deeper and more lasting ways. So, while the language of crisis may serve as a useful catalyst for action, I think it more helpful and useful to move beyond that sentiment and acknowledge more simply and broadly that we live in remarkably disruptive times.

Disruption often is subtle and less obvious than crisis. And unlike crisis, it is not so easily time-stamped. Disruptive forces can take years to develop and fully play out. While not always experienced as a crisis, they can be every bit as life changing. Disruptive periods generally are characterized by significant contextual change. What worked before or what we thought before no longer yields successful results or is no longer true. Think of it as curve bending or trajectory change. Disruption very often challenges long-held assumptions and operating practices and typically demands a structural rather than a symptomatic response. From the standpoint of an organization—any organization—two things become important during disruptive periods: determining how unsettling the disruptive forces actually are to you and then finding opportunity in the disruption.

What has any of this to do with higher education? Nearly all colleges and universities today must address three important disruptive forces that had fully emerged by 2010 and have intensified since then: demographic disruption, economic disruption, and values disruption. Each had been brewing and developing for years, and most institutions had to address their effects to varying degrees prior to 2010. However, the pace and force of each of the disruptions has accelerated, and the interaction of their effects has intensified the level of challenge we face as institutions and raised the stakes associated with our responses to them. Few colleges and universities will receive a free pass as the key forces of disruption in play today unfold and reshape the marketplace for higher education.

CHAPTER THREE

Demographic Disruption

Opportunity comes to those who put away the disadvantage of family or circumstances and entrust themselves to the future. The point of the American story is simple enough for a child, particularly an immigrant child, to grasp: The past holds no sway in America.

—Richard Rodriguez, *Darling*

College leaders everywhere should pay attention to demography. Paying attention does not require an extensive knowledge of the statistics and research underlying demographic science. That's best left to demographers. It does mean, however, that leaders—presidents, senior staff, and boards of trustees—should have a more-than-basic understanding of the population trends and characteristics in and among their institution's primary student markets. Data and information about how many, who, and where are important because demographic patterns form the base from which all colleges build their enrollment goals and projections.

The good news is that changing population patterns do not emerge overnight. Unlike many other disruptive forces that shape markets and frame decision making, colleges and universities have the luxury of a long lead time, at least eighteen years, to prepare for population change. Demographic changes very often occur in subtle or small year-to-year increments that only over a long period of time become significant. While population changes should be the least surprising of the disruptive forces facing higher education, they also can be the easiest to overlook because at any given moment they may not be noticeable. Consequently, colleges and universities need to pay careful attention not only to annual changes in their student markets but also to changes occurring in those markets over a longer period of time. To waste the lead time granted by population change is to risk being caught unaware at the moment an incremental shift suddenly becomes cumulatively important—the moment we reach a tipping point from which there is no easy return or remedy.

Demographic projections have for years indicated that changes among the traditional-age college population—in number and in characteristic—would have profound effects on colleges and universities across the country. By 2008, small annual population changes that had been developing for decades began to take full effect. The effects of the change will continue to evolve for decades to come, with increasingly dramatic consequences for colleges and universities. Put most simply, as the US population changes, it will be more important than ever for leaders of higher education institutions to have a firm understanding of their students and their markets.

By the Numbers

After rising by nearly 36 percent between 1993–94 and 2008–09, the number of high school graduates in the United States peaked in 2010–11 at 3.4 million, the largest graduating class in the nation's history.[1] This should not have been a surprise to anyone. The number of births in the United States increased by 13 percent between 1981 and 1991 (peaking in 1991, the high point for the 1980 to 2000 period).[2] Fast forward eighteen years and you can get a pretty good understanding of the basic number or trend to expect in high school graduates. Rising numbers of births generally points to higher numbers of graduates eighteen years later. Falling numbers of births generally means lower numbers of graduates later.[3] No complex math here, but it does require attention to a few key data points.

According to the Western Interstate Commission for Higher Education (WICHE), whose projections of state and national high school graduates are the most widely cited, the number of graduates nationally began to decline slowly after 2010–11. WICHE's estimates indicate that the number of graduates will continue to fall through 2013–14, a reflection of the small decline in the number of births in the United States in the mid-1990s. Though this is not a particularly steep drop—the number of graduates is expected to decline by just 5.6 percent between 2010–11 and 2013–14 before slowly beginning to rise again—the recovery period will take years. The total number of high school graduates in the United States is not projected to reach 2010–11 levels again until 2023–24. In the intervening years, barring significant changes in the rate of high school completion, we should expect little change in the total number of high school graduates, and thus little change in the total market for traditional-age college students.[4]

College enrollment, of course, does not simply reflect the number of people in a market but also the rate at which they attend college. Postsecondary enrollment in the United States between 1993 and 2008 was fueled not only by rising numbers of high school graduates but also by rising high school–to–college participation rates, which climbed steadily and significantly from the early 1980s through the early years of the new century. By 2004, though, college participation rates among recent high school graduates had leveled off, albeit at very high levels. They have grown only nominally since then. It is not at all clear that the historically high rates will either rise naturally or by inducement from colleges and universities or other market forces.

Like any production function, it will be much more difficult to raise college participation rates from high current levels than it was to drive them up from lower levels. Colleges and universities already have captured the largest share of the high school graduates most likely to pursue a postsecondary education and would need to turn their attention and resources to those who historically have never enrolled (nor had the opportunity to enroll) to boost participation rates further. Those efforts would add significantly to human and social capital development but also would require significant investments in college preparation and access, as well as new recruitment and institutional support strategies for new populations. The alternative scenario—directing no additional attention to increasing college participation rates—points to a more challenging marketplace: if high school–to–college participation rates do not grow as the number of high school graduates contracts, or if they shrink from current levels, the marketplace for traditional-age students in higher education will become more congested, more competitive, and almost surely less predictable.

The shallow, bathtub-like trajectory projected for high school graduates follows nearly two decades of uninterrupted annual growth, to which most colleges and universities across the country became accustomed. The expanding traditional-age market provided ready opportunities to either maintain or increase undergraduate enrollment at many institutions. But the trend line has reversed, or at least stopped its climb, and few institutions will be able to rely on population growth dividends to sustain or increase their

Market highs and lows are hardly unusual. The history of American higher education has been continuously shaped and influenced by them. The question, though, is how well institutions prepare operationally for peaks and valleys. It generally does not make business sense to build out to a market peak when the valley to follow is plainly evident. Building our human, programmatic, and physical infrastructure to the peak of an enrollment crest may seem appropriate as the trajectory moves upward, but it increases operational risk and exposure when markets are no longer expanding or are shrinking. The same kind of thinking works in reverse, too. To forgo market opportunity simply because of an aversion to risk can create significant opportunity costs that can stunt the student experience and limit institutional potential. In the end, colleges and universities should develop plans and investments in the context of sustainable market development, which requires an investment in knowing how markets are evolving and changing.

enrollment—a change that will present different challenges in different parts of the country.

The Illusion of Demand

As the economic, social, and cultural returns to higher education have risen, demand for college also has risen. More students go to college, and they consider more options, than ever before. Even with a shrinking number of traditional-age students and even in challenging economic times, the still tremendous returns to college and the lack of a credible alternative to the experience and the credential mean that demand for postsecondary education likely will remain very strong, which is good news for colleges and universities everywhere. However, institutional leaders must take caution to avoid falling prey to the illusion of demand—the mirage effect associated with seemingly rising interest in spite of market conditions that would suggest otherwise.

Two axioms are absolutely true when it comes to college admission: if you do not apply to a particular college, it is nearly certain you will not enroll there, and not all demand is created equal. The first is self-evident. The second is too often overlooked.

The chase to build larger applicant pools, aided by technology that has vastly simplified the application process and expanded colleges' ability to reach many more students economically, has changed the meaning of demand. Online tools like the Common Application website and prepopulated "fast applications" have made it easier than ever for students to apply to college today. Many institutions have simplified the process even further by reducing or eliminating application fees. In addition, colleges have in recent years become enrollment marketing machines, using mass-market tools crafted and perfected by retail or political operations to cheaply and efficiently reach extraordinary numbers of prospective students. An increasing number of colleges and universities manage enrollment risk not through yield strategies on the back end of the process but rather with demand strategies at the front end of the process designed to create huge applicant pools (which, in theory at least, can be large enough to cover risks associated with declining yield).

Students today, particularly high-achieving students, can and do consider many more institutions than their predecessors—making "real" demand much more difficult to interpret. Though the number of high school graduates has already begun to decline, the number of colleges to which students apply continues to rise, an indicator of how students and their families hedge their admission bets as well as a sign of the reach and effectiveness of contemporary college admission marketing. In 1990, several years before the full-scale commercial development of the Internet, one-quarter of all first-time new entering students attending four-year colleges nationally applied to just one institution and only 4 in 10 applied to more than three. A decade earlier, nearly one-third of new students applied to only one college or university. By 2012, two-thirds of all new entering four-year college students submitted applications to at least three different institutions; only 13 percent applied to only one.[5]

As the number of applications for admission to college has risen, our ability to predict the outcome has declined or at least gotten more complicated, a change reflected in sharply falling yield rates at many institutions. While an admission application is a hopeful sign for any institution, it is not by itself an expression of true or deep interest on the part of the student. It more closely resembles speed dating. More importantly, irrespective of the number of applications a student submits (and the number of institutions to which she or he is accepted), that student will ultimately select and enroll at only one. In other words, unlike shopping at Target or Wal-Mart, where I can choose to buy jeans at one and milk at the other in the same afternoon, college enrollment by and large remains a binary, winner-takes-all proposition: I must choose one place and not another.[6] Transferring to another institution is, of course, an option, but transfer costs can be high in terms of effort, personal circumstances, and the opportunity cost of lost time and academic credit.[7]

The choice of a college, then, is singularly consequential to the student as well as to the winning and losing institution. For every institution that will bask in the glow of admission success in the coming years, another will be forced to consider the wreckage of a seemingly strong market position gone awry. If our applications were up so much in the spring, why did we fare so poorly by the fall? The tools of mass marketing, combined with rising demand, have made predictive uncertainty the new normal, and a more difficult new normal in a numerically shrinking or flat market.

The shrinking pool of traditional-age students raises the institutional stakes associated with winning and losing even further. There are 1,000 *more* degree-granting colleges and universities today than there were in 1996.[8] The crowded and growing postsecondary marketplace has already contributed to competitive pressures at many institutions, even when enrollment was growing. A flat or zero-sum market or, worse, a declining market, will add fuel to already intense competition. If the costs of winning under those circumstances are high, the costs of losing are even higher in a winner-takes-all contest. Barring collaborative market behavior currently forbidden by federal law as collusive, there will be no end to the competitive stakes game for most institutions.

We can decry rush-to-the-bottom pricing practices or the so-called amenity wars, but much like negative political campaign ads, as long as those strategies yield a seemingly positive result, they will continue as widely practiced market tactics. Price is the most malleable and powerful tool most institutions have in their market arsenal. That colleges manipulate it as much as they do should not be at all surprising. Widespread price manipulation is characteristic of a crowded, competitive marketplace shaped by binary purchase choices. In a high-stakes game, individual institutions will fight as hard as they can with the best tools they have available to achieve their objectives.

For students and their families the story is quite different and, whether they know it or not, decidedly more upbeat. The changing marketplace clearly presents them with new college opportunities, shifting the balance of power from seller to buyer. Oft-repeated tales of students who receive college rejection letters in spite of 4.0 grade point averages, high board scores, and

> A shrinking marketplace is a buyer's marketplace, one in which institutions need students more than the students may need a particular institution—a notion families are increasingly likely to embrace and one college and university leaders can ill afford to forget. The shifting balance of market power will embolden those shopping for college on price and will contribute to rising expectations for net price negotiation.

extraordinary high school vitae are more myth than reality, generally true only at a small number of extraordinarily selective private and public colleges and universities. Most institutions have neither widespread brand recognition nor the luxury of excess demand. Questions about whether those institutions "make their class" most often trump questions of who is in the class.

Changing Places

Location, location, location. The mantra of real estate agents everywhere. When it comes to buying or selling a home, place is as important as price, product, and promotion. As it turns out, the same is true when thinking about student markets for higher education. Where an institution calls home is important because regional demographic patterns and trends shape the market opportunity or challenge for the vast majority of colleges and universities in the United States. While national projections of high school graduates do not suggest a significant change in the size of the traditional-age college market, regional patterns and trends cast a much different picture—indicating that opportunity and challenge are highly differentiated by place.

Since America's founding, Americans have had an almost nomadic sense of movement, most of it to the west and south. Whether this has been in search of opportunity or simply more temperate comfort, geographic stasis is not part of our national history or cultural DNA. In 2010, just 59 percent of all Americans resided in the state in which they were born. Roots are deepest in the Northeast and Midwest, colder climate notwithstanding. Two-thirds of all people living in those regions were born in the state in which they now live. By comparison, only 53 percent of all people living in the South or the West were born in the states they live in today (a number influenced both by migration within the country as well as immigration to the country).[9]

The cries of "Westward, ho!" that reshaped the geographic landscape of the United States in the nineteenth century still echo today, though they now also include the South.[10] In 1940, nearly 6 in 10 Americans lived in the northern tier of states stretching from the Dakotas in the West across the Great Lakes region and northeast from Pennsylvania to Maine. New York, Pennsylvania, Ohio, and Illinois collectively provided 29 percent of the nation's total population that year. World War II reshuffled the population deck, and the flight west and south accelerated. By 1960, the populations of California and Florida each had more than doubled and nearly half of all Americans lived in southern or western states. Fast forward to 2012, and the geographic transformation is complete.[11] Today, fully 60 percent of all Americans live in the West or the South. Since 1940, the population of California has grown by more than five times, Texas by more than four times, and Florida by ten times. More than one-quarter of all Americans today live in one of those three states.

Geographic population trends should be more than a source of passing academic interest or weird fascination. They have tremendous implications for enrollment because they locally, regionally, and nationally shape the markets and market opportunities for the vast majority of American colleges and universities. Not surprisingly, geographic changes occurring in the broad population also are playing out in regional changes occurring among high school graduates—changes which will shape and reshape the enrollment outlook for colleges across the country.

Go West, and South!

Every traditional-age student who will begin college in the next twelve years is already enrolled in school somewhere. In the intervening years, it will be more important than ever to closely monitor the accelerating geographic changes occurring among the traditional-age college population.

In 1980–81, the number of high school graduates in the country was split nearly evenly between western and southern states and midwestern and eastern states.[12] Twenty years later that picture had changed dramatically, a reflection of the changes that occurred in the broad US population over the same time period. By 2000–01, the proportion of high school graduates coming from western or southern states had risen to nearly 58 percent. The number graduating from southern states changed little over the period, but the number of high school graduates from western states rocketed upward, growing by nearly 24 percent.[13] The picture was far different in the Northeast and Midwest, where the number of high school graduates fell by 23 percent and 18 percent, respectively.

The geographic gaps created then remain today. Though the numbers of high school graduates have increased in every region of the country in the last decade, they have risen slightly faster in the West and South than in the Midwest or Northeast. In 2012–13, western and southern states were expected to provide 60 percent of the nation's high school graduates.

The geographic center of the nation's youth will continue to edge westward and south over the next decade, albeit more slowly than in prior years. By 2022–23, 61 percent of the nation's high school graduates will hail from those regions.[14] The South alone will be home to 35 percent of all high school graduates in the United States, with the most significant growth expected in Texas, Georgia, North Carolina, and Florida. The number of graduates in the West is expected to rise by 6 percent between its trough in 2013–14 and 2022–23. While graduate numbers will remain essentially stable in the Midwest over the next decade, the outlook in the Northeast is not at all optimistic. Continuing a long trend of decline, the number of high school graduates in the Northeast will fall nearly continuously until 2022–23, requiring that more colleges in the region mine new markets in new places to maintain their enrollment.

The Temple of Their Familiar

Young adults often are portrayed, mythologized really, as footloose and fancy-free travelers anxious to leave the confines of home and their parents' rules for far-flung places in search of opportunity and freedom. It is a pleasant enough story, one that suggests adventure and a particular kind of aspiration, reminiscent of the explorers and pioneers who fill the pages of history books. However, like so many other colorful tales, it is also, by and large, untrue.

Most college enrollment is local. Most students buy what they know, and what they know best (or believe they know best) typically is close to home. The vast majority of new entering students who enroll at four-year colleges and universities nationally travel fewer than 500 miles to attend school, and more than half travel less than 100 miles from bedroom to dorm room.[15] For many young people moving out on their own for the first time, there really is no place like proximity to home.

Institution type and admission selectivity play a significant role in the geographic profile of new students. Students attending large universities or highly selective colleges and universities, public or private, typically travel much farther distances than those attending smaller or less selective institutions. For example, nearly half of all students attending the most selective private universities in the country, travel more than 500 miles from home to school, and three-quarters travel more than 100 miles. But students at those colleges represent only a small share of all new students in the United States, and their experience is not the norm. More than half of all first-time new entering students attending nonselective four-year public or private colleges and universities travel fewer than 50 miles to school.[16] Home matters.

This is not a new phenomenon. Even as admission operations reach farther afield with more zeal than ever before to attract students, including much more intensive efforts to enroll international students, the percentage of new students choosing to enroll at a four-year college or university that is more than 100 miles from home is not higher today than it was in 1970, and for students attending four-year colleges (not universities), it is considerably lower.[17] In fall 2012, fewer than 40 percent of all new entering students attending public and private four-year colleges in the United States traveled more than 100 miles to school. Never have more than 1 in 7 new entering students across all four-year colleges and universities traveled over 500 miles to go to college.

While most college students choose to stay close to home, few historically have cited that as an important reason for selecting a particular college and most do not live at home with their parents. According to UCLA's Higher Education Research Institute survey, *The American Freshman*, three-quarters of all first-time new entering college students in fall 2012 who enrolled at baccalaureate institutions nationally lived in residence halls on campus. Only 1 in 5 cited proximity to home as a "very important" factor in their college choice.[18] The percentage of new students pointing to home as an important factor in their college decision has risen since the mid-1980s (when it was only 15%), but even so, the overwhelming majority of new college students today do not identify proximity to home as a top-of-mind criterion in their college selection process. Their behavior, though, belies their intention. Whether they cite it as a factor or not, it is clear that most students—and likely most of their parents—prefer the security of a comfortable day's drive or less between home and college, particularly at an important transitional point in their life. Not everyone has the heart of a pioneer.

That most students do not travel far to college raises the admission stakes associated with regional demographic trends. While demography may not be destiny, geographic choice patterns clearly influence market opportunity for most colleges and universities in the United States. Consequently, most institutions need to keep close watch on the in-state and in-region trends that will shape their enrollment fortune. Put another way, your backyard matters—a lot—and the core of a successful recruitment strategy must begin there.

Institutions located in states where the population is flat or shrinking often must look farther afield to meet their enrollment goals. But even then, enrollment potential is not distributed evenly. The two colleges at which I work are located in Central Minnesota, a region of the country that sends a very high percentage of its high school graduates to college (the good news) but whose traditional-age college population is flat or declining (the bad news). While the College of Saint Benedict and Saint John's University draw the majority of their students from Minnesota and the Upper Midwest, we increasingly must look outside of our region for new students. However, if I draw a line 500 miles out from our location in Central Minnesota, the outer limit of travel for most domestic students, we capture only about 10 percent of the nation's total under-age-18 population. Lots of cows and corn. Fewer people. If we were located instead in east-central Pennsylvania, let's say Harrisburg to make this interesting, that same 500-mile radius would include almost 30 percent of the nation's young population. Any college could—and should—draw a similar kind of map to get a basic and beginning understanding of their enrollment opportunity.

Think Locally, Act Globally

Of course, not all undergraduate students hail from the United States. Though international students have long comprised a significant percentage of graduate and professional enrollments in the United States, efforts to enroll more undergraduate students from across the globe have intensified at colleges and universities around the country in recent years. Whether approached as a way to weather difficulty in domestic enrollment markets or to introduce more cultural diversity on campus, undergraduate international student recruitment today receives more attention than ever before.

While the overall enrollment numbers suggest impressive growth and op-portunity, a closer look paints a less clear picture. Between fall 2000 and fall 2012, the number of undergraduate international students enrolled at degree-granting two-year and four-year institutions in the United States rose by more than 50 percent, increasing from 288,000 to 450,000 over the twelve-year time span.[19] The total number of undergraduate international students attending US colleges has risen every year since 2005. But those broad num-bers provide an incomplete story for purposes of assessing market oppor-tunity. In spite of the significant enrollment growth over the last decade, international students still made up only 2.5 percent of all undergraduates in the United States in fall 2012, only slightly higher than their share in fall 2000. While those figures certainly would not describe the trend at every institution in the country, they do suggest that at most colleges and univer-sities in the United States international students provide only a small share of total undergraduate enrollment.

In addition, while "international" may suggest global, the majority of in-ternational students studying in the United States come from just three countries: China, which provides more than 30 percent of all international students enrolled in the United States; India, which provides 12 percent of all international students; and South Korea, which provides nearly 8 percent of all international students.[20] Together those nations provide almost half of all international undergraduate and graduate students enrolled at US colleges and universities today. In total, 6 in 10 international students in the United States come from eastern or southeastern Asia or the Indian subcontinent. No other region of the globe is as populous, and no other region sends even close to as many students to study in the United States. It remains to be seen whether those nations will continue to send as many students abroad for their undergraduate or graduate degrees as they increase their investments in their own higher education infrastructure.

More important than the raw numbers or the overall market size, a deci-sion to ramp up enrollment of international students demands a simultane-ous commitment to providing the academic and student support services those students require. How will we address language issues? What kind of specialized academic advising will we offer to international students? How will we integrate international students into the life and fabric of the campus so they don't simply become an isolated subculture? These questions are best answered before recruitment of international students begins. In addition, an effort to enroll more international students obliges an institution to provide the support those students need to navigate federal immigration requirements, helping them to maintain the terms and conditions of their nonimmigrant student status.[21]

There are more than 200 million young people aged 15 to 24 in China alone, surely the largest single market of college-age students in the world.[22] It is tempting and easy to assert that enrollment of perhaps a few dozen of those millions at my institution ought to be an attainable goal each year. However, while international student enrollment surely represents an opportunity for many colleges and universities in the United States, that opportunity cannot be realized without an understanding of why a particular institution might be attractive to students from outside of the United States. And it will not come without cost. In addition to providing prospective international students with a compelling reason to attend my college or university, reaching and maintaining an enrollment goal also demands that we create the human and programmatic infrastructure to ensure their well-being and success. Anything short of either does little more than create conditions for failure.

Strategic enrollment plans typically identify a national enrollment target or aspiration, and increasingly an international goal, too. Demographic changes within the United States demand that kind of thinking. However, those plans must rest on a clear-eyed understanding of the institution's geographic place in the market—whom you historically have attracted and a realistic assessment of whom you might be able to attract in the future and why. Can enrollment of international students provide at least a part of the solution to regional demographic change and uncertainty? Done well, absolutely. However, enrollment success from afar requires that institutional leaders identify a compelling advantage associated with their institution, one that clearly and meaningfully differentiates them from all of the other closer-to-home choices the student has and one that minimizes concerns typically associated with long-distance travel.

Changing Faces

Mitt Romney captured 59 percent of the white vote in the 2012 presidential election.[23] He garnered a 20-percentage-point margin of victory over President Obama, likely the largest percentage ever for a single candidate among white voters. In any other election in American history, that margin of victory among white voters surely would have propelled Romney to the Oval Office. But in 2012, he lost. And he lost handily, in both the Electoral College and the popular vote.

The particular politics of race and ethnicity aside, the 2012 presidential election says much about the changing face of America. Though he lost the white vote by a wide margin, President Obama received 93 percent of the black vote, 71 percent of the Hispanic vote, and 73 percent of the Asian vote. Democrats had captured large percentages of the nonwhite vote in prior presidential elections, but the subpopulations were not large enough to swing the outcome. They are now, and they will be for decades to come.

The growing racial and ethnic diversity of the US population, and its impact on politics, economics, and culture, should not come as a surprise. The trend toward increasing diversity has been building for years. Between 2000 and 2010, the nation's minority population[24] increased by 29 percent, rising from nearly 87 million to 112 million. The number of white, non-Hispanic Americans grew by just 1 percent over the decade.[25] Led by extraordinary growth in the Hispanic population, the nonwhite population in the United States has more than doubled in the last thirty years. By 2010, people of color comprised 36 percent of the nation's total population, up from 31 percent in 2000 and just 20 percent in 1980.

The trend to increasing racial and ethnic diversity is not a blip on the demographic radar. It is long-term and likely permanent. The population of color in the United States is both younger and growing more rapidly than the white population. In 2012, the US Census Bureau reported that, for the first time in American history, more than half of the nation's population under age 1 was nonwhite, a sign of significant cultural and social change yet to come.[26] Last year, young people of color made up more than 45 percent of all Americans under age 18 (compared to just 25% of those aged 45 and older).[27]

According to WICHE projections, all of the growth in high school graduates nationally between 2013 and 2023 will occur among young people of color.[28] The number of white high school graduates will drop by more than 8 percent over the ten-year period (it had already fallen by 5% in the prior

For colleges and universities everywhere, the changing racial and ethnic profile of America's young population is more interesting and certainly more compelling and important than basic demographic projections. Increasing racial, ethnic, and cultural diversity presents us with new enrollment opportunities but also with new enrollment challenges. Irrespective of the choices higher education leaders make or the strategies they employ, the changing US population will shape and drive college enrollment for years to come.

ten-year period), while the number of graduates of color will collectively rise by nearly 19 percent. By 2023, graduates of color will represent nearly half of all high school graduates in the country, up from one-third in 2003. The trend will repeat itself in every region of the country. Young people of color will make up the majority of graduates in both the West (where they already comprise a majority) and the South by 2023, and their share of all graduates will rise to 28 percent in the Midwest (up from 24% in 2013) and to 39 percent in the Northeast (up from 34% in 2013).

While the big numbers are interesting, it is more important to pay close attention to what is happening among subpopulations. The number of black high school graduates, who until 2008 made up the largest group of non-white graduates in the country, is expected to decline by 6 percent between 2013 and 2023 before essentially stabilizing. The number of American Indian or Alaskan Native graduates will grow slightly, but consistently will continue to represent only 1 percent of all high school graduates in the country.[29]

The most significant growth will occur among Asian and Hispanic students, with the lion's share of the change propelled by the continued explosive growth in the Hispanic population. Over the next ten years, the number of Asian high school graduates in the United States will grow by nearly 59,000, a gain of 33 percent. Their share of all graduates will rise from 5 percent in 2013 to 8 percent by 2023. Significant as that change is, it will pale in comparison to the change among Hispanic graduates over the same period. Between 2013 and 2023, the number of Hispanic high school graduates nationally will explode, projected to rise by 188,000. By 2023, Hispanic graduates are expected to make up one-quarter of all high school graduates in the country, double their share at the beginning of the century. Hispanic students already make up the largest share of graduates of color. Their plurality will widen to a majority by 2019.

As the nation's population continues to change, our understanding of the term "underrepresented" likely will change, too, at least as it relates to racial and ethnic diversity. Students of color no longer represent a small numeric minority of all students, or even a minority at all in some places (like California, Texas, and Florida). Similar to the change in the electorate, the entire market for traditional-age students is more racially and ethnically diverse than it ever has been. And it will become significantly more so. For purposes of institutional planning, these are not changes occurring on the margin that require no more than fleeting or episodic or create-a-targeted-program attention. Diversity defines the new marketplace for higher education, and new enrollment strategies must reflect that fact. Colleges and universities that do not figure out how to enroll and retain the rising number of students of color not only will find it increasingly difficult to meet their enrollment goals but also will put themselves at risk of becoming little more than social anachronisms.

Bienvenido al Futuro de los Estados Unidos

The extraordinary growth in the Hispanic population deserves additional attention. It is not a phenomenon limited to a single area of the country, or even exclusively to particular types of places. Its effects have been and will continue to be felt everywhere.

I live in a small town in the geographic center of Minnesota, population approximately 4,000. The community has a deep and closely held sense of its German heritage. Many of my neighbors have family histories in the area that date to the mid- and late nineteenth-century immigration of their ancestors. Few people, either in the community or outside of it, would view Cold Spring, Minnesota, as particularly emblematic of the increasingly Hispanic face of America. But it is.

While the largest numeric growth in the US Hispanic population has occurred in California, Texas, and other southern states, tremendous demographic changes are playing out in big and small communities all across the country. In my small town in Central Minnesota, enrollment of Hispanic children in our local elementary and secondary schools grew by 52 percent between 2006 and 2012.[30] Similar to trends in school districts in urban and rural communities around the country, the number of white students in Cold Spring area schools fell by nearly 16 percent over the same time period. Today, Latino children represent more than 10 percent of all children in grades K through 4 in our public schools, compared to less than 2 percent a decade earlier. Small numbers in a small town, to be sure, but rapid change in a community that for over one hundred years had experienced little if any real ethnic change. Similar changes are occurring in towns and cities, large and small, across the nation.

There are 50 million people of Hispanic descent in the United States today, nearly equal to the sum total of the nation's black and Asian populations (53 million).[31] The number of Hispanics in the United States rose by an astonishing 43 percent between 2000 and 2010. More than half of the nation's total population growth over the decade was provided by Hispanics.

Remarkably, only eight states experienced growth of *less than* 40 percent in their Hispanic population between 2000 and 2010, and twelve states experienced growth of 90 percent or more.[32] By 2010, Hispanics accounted for 16 percent of the total US population.[33] Although it has often been erroneously portrayed otherwise on talk radio and during debates on immigration reform, the majority of Hispanics in the United States—63 percent—were born here, and the number and proportion born here are rising.[34]

The growing Hispanic population in the United States is a phenomenon of the young, not the old. The median age of Hispanic Americans in 2011 was just 27, nearly half a generation younger than the US population as a whole (whose median age was 37).[35] Hispanic births made up nearly one-quarter of all newborns in the country in 2011.[36] Children grow up, and rising numbers of births eventually lead to rising school enrollment. In 2009, more than 1 in 5 elementary and secondary school children in America were Hispanic.[37] The rapidly growing Hispanic population in the United States will drive and shape school enrollment across the country—including enrollment at colleges and universities—for years to come.

Clearly, the train of demographic change has left the station. At a minimum, the rapid growth in the Hispanic population should encourage us to quickly develop an understanding of the enrollment potential and prospects of Hispanic young people in our colleges and universities. Young Hispanic Americans clearly recognize the opportunities associated with college. Research conducted by the Pew Research Hispanic Center found that nearly 9 in 10 Hispanics aged 16 to 25 believe that a college education is necessary to get ahead in life. More than three-quarters of them reported that their parents believe that going to college is the most important thing for them to do after completing high school.[38]

Reflecting both the rapid growth in population and Hispanic students' postsecondary aspirations, their enrollment has risen sharply in recent years. Between 2007 and 2012, the number of undergraduate Hispanic students in the United States rose by 44 percent, significantly faster than any other racial or ethnic group, and even faster than international student enrollment.[39] By 2012, Hispanics made up 16 percent of all undergraduate students in the country, compared to 12.5 percent just five years earlier. The number and proportion will continue to rise throughout the next decade.

But enrolling in college and completing a college degree are two different things. Fewer than half of all 18- to 25-year-old Hispanics indicate that they plan to complete a bachelor's degree or more (compared to 60% of all similar-aged young people). Immigrants were less than half as likely as those born in the United States to say they planned to even attend college.[40] Lower rates of degree attainment result, in part, from lower rates of enrollment at four-year colleges. In fall 2012, only 48 percent of all Hispanic undergraduates were enrolled at four-year institutions, compared to more than 60 percent of white and Asian undergraduates.[41] Among those who do enroll at four-year institutions, Hispanic and black students complete at far lower rates than white and Asian students. Only half of all Hispanic students enrolled at four-year institutions, and less than 40 percent of black students, earn their baccalaureate degrees in six years or less, compared to 6 in 10 white students and two-thirds of Asian students.[42] The losses in human and financial capital associated with nonenrollment and noncompletion will be neither acceptable nor sustainable as the nation's demographic profile continues to change.

Fewer than one-quarter of all Hispanics in the United States aged 25 to 29 have earned a college degree of some kind, and only 15 percent have completed a four-year degree—both rates of attainment significantly lower than rates for the same age population as a whole (43% of all 25- to 29-year-olds have completed a two-year or four-year degree, with one-third earning a four-year degree).[43]

The comparatively low rates of four-year college enrollment and baccalaureate degree attainment among young Hispanics surely are influenced by a variety of social, cultural, and economic factors and conditions not subject to quick or easy solutions. Consequently, while the growing Hispanic population presents a clear enrollment opportunity for colleges and universities across the country—and likely an enrollment imperative—four-year colleges and universities often will face significant challenges converting aspiration to matriculation and success.

Beyond the Numbers

Important as the big numbers are, demography is not simply a numbers game. The characteristics of the people and populations who comprise the figures are important. And those characteristics—particularly the economic characteristics of families—often are not benign in terms of educational opportunity.

A college education is widely and rightly understood as a prospect-widening experience. It historically has provided students from all backgrounds and means with access to social, cultural, and economic opportunities they otherwise might not have had without it. College today has become a critical gateway for access to the middle class, a fact well understood by students and families across America. For our part, colleges and universities typically seek to provide an experience intended to support and develop all of the students we enroll, irrespective of the family circumstances from which they come. In that sense, a postsecondary education is a powerful social equalizer, an entryway to shared opportunity—a position that carries with it an extraordinary social responsibility.

Unfortunately, while a college education creates a pathway for career success and personal fulfillment, the ability to enroll in college to take advantage of that opportunity very often is influenced, and delimited, by economics, most importantly family income. Income often is an unpleasant and difficult subject to discuss. We prefer to set our sights on the loftier and more conversationally comfortable issue of equity—that irrespective of means, everyone in America who sets their mind and effort to it can succeed economically. That's an easy sentiment in which to believe among those who are already economically secure but much more difficult for those who are not. While money may not be able to buy love or happiness, it clearly buys access to the American dream and to a modicum of security simply unknown to those who do not have it.

There are striking and consequential differences in family income by race and ethnicity, differences that occasionally have narrowed but historically have persisted. In 2012, the median income for non-Hispanic white and Asian families with school-age children (which includes children aged 6 to 17) was nearly double the median for similar black and Hispanic families.[44] The differences do not simply occur at the median but are reflected throughout the income distribution.

More than 9 percent of all white and Asian families report incomes in excess of $200,000—high incomes by almost any definition for purposes of college access—compared to fewer than 2 percent of all black and Hispanic families. On the other end of the income spectrum, approximately half of all Hispanic and black families with school-age children report incomes below $40,000, a level of income that would make the vast majority of them eligible for federal Pell Grants, compared to fewer than one-quarter of white and Asian families. Put another way, white and Asian students are four times more likely than black or Hispanic students to come from families who have the wherewithal to pay for college anywhere. On the other hand, black and

Hispanic students are more than twice as likely as white or Asian students to come from families who will struggle to pay for college anywhere.

Family income plays a powerful role influencing educational opportunity, irrespective of race or ethnicity. Though college participation rates have risen for students of all incomes since the 1970s (growing fastest among those with the lowest incomes), they remain nearly two times higher for those in the top income quartile than for those in the bottom quartile. In 2011, more than 80 percent of all dependent 18- to 24-year-olds in the top income quartile, which included students from families with incomes over $104,750, were enrolled in college, compared to less than 45 percent of those with incomes in the bottom quartile (students from families with incomes below $33,283).[45]

If we layer college participation and income data with the demographic changes projected for the next decade, the postsecondary access and opportunity challenges become clear. Questions of whether to go to college, where to go to college, and how to pay for college will become increasingly immediate and daunting for a rising share of the traditional-age population. They present equally daunting challenges to college and university leaders and public policy makers, as well. In 2012, 37 percent of all black and Hispanic families with school-age children reported incomes below $30,000. Only 14 percent had incomes over $100,000—where college-going rates are highest among people of all races and ethnicities.[46]

Barring significant changes in high school progression, high school completion, or family income, many of these lower income students will have limited access to college, particularly at four-year colleges and universities. Successful enrollment of lower-income students will require substantial new investments in student financial aid, well beyond what many institutions currently have committed. Colleges and universities, as well as policy makers, must decide now how they will address these challenges. The social and economic consequences of inaction or insufficient action will have lasting consequences. The promise of the new demography in America cannot be realized without long-term commitments to preparation, achievement, and academic and financial support.

CHAPTER FOUR

Economic Disruption

An economist is a man that can tell you anything. His guess is liable to be as good as anybody else's, too.

—Will Rogers

Without doubt, the price of college weighs heavily on families' minds. Most of the conversations I have about college with friends or the families of prospective students do not begin with questions about majors or activities or life on campus. They go straight to price. Where can I find more information about scholarships? How much should we borrow for college? Where can I get help with my financial aid application? We just aren't sure we can swing that price. If we choose this college for our son, how will we pay for our daughter's college later? And so on. Real questions, earnestly expressed. The dream of attending a college often bumps uncomfortably against the reality of paying for it. This is true for families across the income spectrum. Rising before the Great Recession, but white hot in the years since, fear about paying for college is pervasive today and is the single most disruptive force college and university leaders face as we plan for the future of our institutions.

Public sentiment about the value of going to college and the price of college is unambiguous. On the one hand, an overwhelming majority of Americans view a college education as essential in today's world. More than 7 in 10 believe that having an education beyond high school is very important to a person's financial security.[1] Nearly 8 in 10 say that having a college education is either very important or extremely important in helping young people succeed today.[2] Among current college students and their parents, 70 percent strongly agree that a college degree is more important now than it used to be, and more than 80 percent regard it as an investment in the future.[3] All good news, as well as an accurate reflection of the economic value of a post-secondary education. What colleges and universities do is highly valued, even prized.

On the other hand, though, Americans are skeptical and concerned about the economics of higher education and have been for a long time. In 2011, three-quarters of all Americans described college costs today as unafford-able for most people—nearly identical to public sentiment twenty years ear-lier.[4] Parents of current students are particularly concerned about rising col-lege prices and the assistance required to help pay for it. More than 6 in 10 college parents in 2012 indicated that they were worried about rising tuition, and nearly half said they worry that scholarships and grants for their sons and daughters will be less available in the future.[5] At my institutions, only 16 percent of the parents of our enrolled first-year students in fall 2012 indi-cated that they were confident they would have enough money for their son or daughter to complete their education at the College of Saint Benedict or Saint John's University. Nearly 30 percent said they had major concerns about their ability to pay for their son or daughter's education. The recession appears to have had no discernible impact on their worry about college costs. A similar percentage of Saint Benedict and Saint John's parents in 2008 said they had major concerns about their ability to pay for college. Whether that is good news (it hasn't gotten worse) or bad news (it hasn't gotten better, either) is not the point. The bottom line is that most families feel, and have felt for some time, the squeeze of the rising price of college.

Likely reflecting their apprehension about high and rising college costs, students and parents alike most often view the value of college through the lens of the economic, rather than the developmental, return it offers. Only one-quarter strongly agreed they would go to college or send their child to college for the intellectual or social experience independent of the earnings potential associated with the degree.[6] Flipping an old aphorism, the prevailing sentiment in selecting a college today is "no return, no deposit."

What are colleges and universities to make of the economic anxiety that prevails among students and parents? When thinking about the price of college, all institutions can place their students in one of three basic economic groups:

1. *The clearly in need of financial aid.* These are students for whom the total price of attendance at an institution before financial aid—inclusive of tuition, fees, room, board, and other recognized costs—is equal to half or more of their family income. These students almost always require at least some amount of financial assistance in the form of need-based grant aid, student employment, and student loans to make their enrollment possible. Because it is pegged to the total cost of attendance, this definition typically extends well beyond the lowest-income students, often reaching middle-income and upper-middle-income students and, at the highest-priced institutions, even families who by any other economic definition would be considered upper-income. At my institutions, for example, each with a comprehensive cost of attendance of approximately $45,000 in 2012–13, the clearly needy included all of our students with family incomes below $90,000—an income threshold that last year would have included two-thirds of all American families with children. Qualification for financial aid also is influenced by the number of children in the family and particularly the number enrolled in college. More children or more in college typically raises the threshold for financial need.

2. *The clearly full-pay.* These are students for whom the price of college is not an issue, at least on paper. It does not mean they are insensitive to price, only that they typically have the means or access to the means to pay for their daughter or son's college education without additional financial assistance. To fit within this category, the comprehensive price of attendance at an institution should not exceed 20 percent to 25 percent of their annual family income. A simpler way to broadly identify these families is to set the income threshold at $200,000, a high enough mark to ensure full-pay status most of the time at most colleges and universities in the country (assuming, of course, that these families do not have many children or more than two in college at the same time, all other things remaining equal). Though full-pay students are the most hunted and overrecruited group of students in American higher education, only 6 percent of all American families with children met or exceeded the $200,000 income threshold in 2011. While students from high-income families are overrepresented at baccalaure-

ate institutions in the United States—they comprised 12 percent of all first-time, full-time new entering students in fall 2012[7]—there simply are not enough of them to fill the seats of all of the colleges and universities who want and need them (and who also believe that these families will willingly and happily pay the full price for their college experience).

3. *The ambiguously needy or wealthy.* Principally students from families who would describe themselves as middle-class or upper-middle-class, this group fits into neither of the other two categories. They perceive themselves as neither high-income nor lower-income. They often have the means to live quite comfortably, though they just as often do not believe they have the available resources to pay for a college education without additional assistance. These families typically have incomes between $75,000 and $175,000 and collectively represent about one-third of all American families (and a similar percentage of all baccalaureate students in the United States). While they may have some savings, the amounts saved typically are not enough in combination with their incomes to wholly finance their children's college dreams. Their incomes and assets generally put them above the threshold for federal or state need-based grant aid, which makes them comparatively more reliant on institutionally awarded grants and scholarships and student or family loans. College participation rates are very high among these students and families; they fully embrace the value of college as a gateway to the middle class and a ticket to staying there. And they fully fear the cost of college for their children.

The vast majority of the US population fits into the first and last categories. Students from each of those two groups fill the classroom chairs and residence halls of most four-year colleges and universities in the country. The Great Recession hit them squarely in the pocketbook, and years after the recession's formal end they continue to feel its residual effects. For them, fear and uncertainty remain signature economic emotions, each of which influences the way they view higher education broadly and the way they view individual institutions. Trends associated with four family economic indicators—income, net worth, saving, and unemployment—will continue to influence the higher education landscape and our opportunity in it for years to come. Each shapes the way students and families understand and approach the prospective return on their educational investment.

Losing Ground

When my oldest son was ten years old, he suggested to my wife and me that we get an ATM at home. He had ascertained by observation that money was provided by a machine. You slide a card into a box, punch some numbers on a screen and, voila, out comes spending cash. Kind of like the stork, only financial. Instead of taking the opportunity to provide a lesson in personal money management, I simply said then that his mother and I were like an ATM, only we did not require a PIN (though "please" and "thank you" would be appreciated). Now a teenager soon to head off to college, my son recently obtained his driver's license, his passport to social freedom. His perspective on income is quite different these days. Owning a car, his fondest wish, and maintaining and insuring it, requires a steady source of income. His lifestyle and lifestyle choices depend on his ability to secure a job and make money. He now knows that what comes out of the ATM is a function of what goes in.

As my son has newly discovered, most people assess their financial situation and wherewithal first through the lens of their income. Am I earning enough money to make the monthly payments on this vehicle or home, to buy these clothes or put this food on the table, to take a vacation this year, or to pay for my son or daughter's education? We are not a nation of great savers, which makes cash flow derived from income king. My income determines not only my purchasing power and freedom but also just as often the way I feel about my social standing. More importantly, it shapes my sense of security or insecurity about the present and the future.

American families have ample reason to worry about their income, particularly as it relates to the rising price of college. The significant economic growth that occurred in the years preceding the 2007 recession did not translate into higher real incomes for most families. Between 2000 and 2007, family incomes by and large kept pace with consumer inflation (which averaged just 2.8% per year during that period). In 2007, inflation-adjusted family income was nearly identical to what it had been in 2000. The recession changed everything. Between 2007 and 2011, real median family income plummeted by more than 8 percent, a trend influenced in large part by the unemployment jump that marked the period. Median income today is similar to what it was in the mid-1990s.[8]

The Great Recession and its aftermath have proved difficult for all types of families but particularly those of most interest to colleges: families with children. Inflation-adjusted incomes for families with children under age 18 fell by more than 8 percent between 2007 and 2012. They have fallen by more than 11 percent since 2000.[9] Family incomes have neither kept pace with inflation nor even fully recovered to prerecession levels since the downturn's end. Flat or falling family income in America reflects the impact of both economic and demographic change. It is among the most challenging issues facing colleges and universities today, and it will influence educational access and opportunity for years to come.

While questions about why the price of college is so high often press on us from outside of our institutions, a common question inside is why we spend so much on financial aid for our students. Do they really need it? Why can't we net more tuition revenue per student? Setting aside for the moment the complexity of financial aid formulas (whose internal workings are understood by few outside of the financial aid office and by almost no families) as well as debates inside higher education about the merits or demerits of non-need-based scholarships and who receives them, the answer is quite simple. Most colleges award a lot of financial aid because for most families college is a remarkably costly experience, particularly in relation to their income. It really is as simple as that.

The financial effort required to pay for college clearly varies significantly by income, but even so it remains an extraordinary investment for the vast majority of American families—an expense unlike any other besides the purchase of a home. In 2012, the average total cost of attendance at public four-year colleges and universities in the United States (inclusive of tuition, fees, and room and board) was equal to more than 25 percent of the income of 60 percent of all American families. The gaps were larger at private colleges and universities, where the total cost of attendance before financial aid exceeded 35 percent of the incomes of 80 percent of all families.[10] It should hardly come as a surprise to college leaders that families blanch at those figures.

Since 2000, the pre–financial aid price of college at both public and private four-year institutions in the United States has increased substantially at all levels of family income but particularly for those in the bottom three income quintiles. More simply, the price of attendance at four-year colleges and universities has risen considerably faster than family income at all levels but especially so for those with the lowest incomes. Though most families today apply for and receive financial aid, they must contend first with the sticker price of attendance. And that most often is a daunting proposition, not least of all because the expense will be incurred for four (and often more) years. Families understand this, perhaps sometimes better than we do on campus.

As families wrestle with the diminished purchasing power of their incomes, it also remains to be seen how or if their spending and saving priorities will change as they consider college options for their children. Downward pressure on college price surely will continue in coming years; it is not simply a passing fad. Moreover, price anxiety just as surely will continue to move upward through higher and higher levels of family income as the price of college rises. That will create for most colleges and universities significant budget, planning, and value challenges and test their twin commitments to access and affordability. At a minimum, the long-term decline and subsequent flattening in family income, in combination with population changes indicating a growing number of lower-income families, suggests that already-growing financial aid budgets at most institutions will continue their inexorable rise.

The rising price of college in relation to income means two things. First, for many families it requires much greater financial effort to pay for college, which raises the stakes associated with their perception and expectation of value at the colleges they consider. Next, from the vantage point of colleges and universities, it elevates the investment and effort required to ensure they remain affordable and accessible, while at the same time providing demonstrable value to students of all family incomes.

The recession packed an income punch from which most families have not yet recovered—a wallop delivered in the form of flat or falling real wage and salary income as well as higher unemployment. It is not clear how family income will fare as the economy continues to improve. The income hole from which they will continue to need to recover is deep, and there is little evidence suggesting a rapid or widespread turnaround in earning potential (particularly while unemployment and underemployment remain high).

There's No Place Like Home

Students and families pay for college from three broad and different pots of resources: current income typically derived from employment, future income in the form of borrowing which must be repaid with future earnings, and past income drawn from assets and earnings on savings. The effective combination of the three, which requires a long-term approach to financing college, can ease the pressure on any single resource as a payment method and broaden college opportunity. Unfortunately, the reality of everyday life often intervenes and conspires to disrupt that simple and neat model. As punishing as the recession was on family incomes, it exacted an even steeper price from net worth and accumulated savings—one that left family balance sheets fragile and considerably more vulnerable to future college expenses.

To be clear, not all of the economic news in recent years has been cause to reach for antacids or pain relief. By early 2013, the stock market losses incurred during the depths of the recession had fully recovered, at least nominally. All of the major financial market indices in the United States had roared back to meet or exceed their prerecession highs. The rapid rebound of financial markets has been one of the few truly positive stories of the post-2009 economic recovery in the United States.

Rising stock market values, reflective of strong corporate earnings and balance sheets, have been very good to publicly traded firms as well as to individuals who had and chose to stick with their stock portfolios through the recession's darkest days. Rising equity values also have been good for college and university investment portfolios and endowment values, both seriously damaged during the recession. As the value of their assets plummeted during the recession, many colleges and universities responded by cutting costs, including in many cases salaries or benefits. Recent growth in endowment and investment values not only provides critical operating income, it also affords at least some hedge against the risk of falling family incomes and diminished ability to pay for college.

But while rising stock market values make great headline news and fodder for chatter on cable business news networks, Wall Street's gains have thus far offered little direct benefit to most people on Main Street. The proportion of American families' directly or indirectly holding stocks has grown substantially since 1992. However, a very large percentage of American families still have no direct stake in financial markets. In 2010, just half of all families in the United States directly or indirectly owned stock in publicly traded companies, down slightly from a peak of 53 percent in 2007, before the recession began. The median value of those holdings totaled just $29,000 in 2010, and the value of those median holdings declined by 18 percent between 2007 and 2010. Not surprisingly, higher-income families are much more likely than those with lower incomes to hold equity assets of one kind or another. Equity holdings are most significant (that is, likely to be in excess of $200,000) only among those with incomes approaching or exceeding $150,000.[11]

The story of the equity boom, positive as it is or seems to be, also in many ways describes the continuing concentration of wealth in America. Among those with stock holdings, the bull market has provided an opportunity for significant financial gain. Many of those families already had significant financial assets and, as a result, could expect access to a very wide range of higher education opportunities. However, for a very large percentage of families, particularly those with the lowest incomes (where the population is growing the fastest), rising stock market values have contributed little to their financial wherewithal and have provided them with no significant new or enhanced opportunities to finance a college education.

While stock indices may not provide a useful proxy to describe the wealth of most American families, home values are a different story. Homes, not stocks, historically have been the primary asset held by most families. Two-thirds of all American families own a home (including three-quarters of all couples with children). In 2010, home value accounted for nearly 30 percent of total family assets in the United States, the largest single component of wealth for a large percentage of families.[12] Prior to the financial reset caused by the Great Recession, it had been an unassailable American presumption—though clearly not an empirical truth—that home prices and home values would always rise, in spite of the adage that "anything too good to be true probably isn't true." Rising home equity over a long period of time provided families with access to capital, in some cases extraordinary access, turning cul-de-sacs into piggy banks and vastly expanding Americans' ability to borrow and spend.

Between 2000 and 2006, the average price of homes in the United States rose by nearly 90 percent, a remarkable increase in a short period of time.[13] The run-up in home values and home equity, in combination with an exuberant lending climate, surely encouraged families to spend and borrow more than they otherwise would have or historically could have. Unfortunately, like so many stories of easy money, what seemed too good to be true in fact ended up too good to be true. Many families learned the very hard way—through foreclosure or immense financial losses—that home values do not always move in one direction. Average home prices in the United States peaked in the first quarter of 2006. By the second quarter of 2009 they had plunged by nearly 31 percent and have been more or less mired at those levels since then (though by early 2013 they began showing signs of real recovery).[14]

It likely will take years to return to the peaks experienced in 2006, in part because the market conditions that allowed the run-up in home prices up to that point were artificial, and financial practices were altered in their wake to try to prevent future bubbles in housing markets. Still, artificially derived or not, plunging home values had a very real impact on family balance sheets. Median home values (not prices) fell by almost 19 percent in real dollars between 2007 and 2010. Worse, median home equity (the difference between the property's worth and the lien against it) fell by 32 percent during and immediately after the recession, dropping from $110,000 in 2007 to just $75,000 in 2010.[15] By early 2012, nearly one-quarter of all homes in the United States with mortgages were "underwater"—meaning the homeowners were holding mortgages worth more than the value of their homes.[16] The underwater rate was nearly five times higher than what historically had been considered normal in a healthy housing market.

In a three-year span, many cul-de-sac piggy banks went belly-up, and an important source of capital, and often a significant part of family financial planning for college, vanished. Today, home equity remains diminished and, in spite of recent recovery, home values remain far below their peak values of less than a decade ago. An important leg of the college financing stool has, for now at least, largely been cut off.

Led by the collapse of home prices and home value, family net worth plummeted during the recession, the median value falling by 39 percent in inflation-adjusted dollars between 2007 and 2010.[17] All types of families in all parts of the country experienced significant losses in net worth, with the notable exception of those with the highest incomes. Among the hardest hit were couples with children (whose net worth declined by 41%), those aged 35 to 44 (whose net worth fell by 54%), and people living in the West (whose net worth, led by the extraordinary collapse of home prices and values in the region, fell by 55%). By 2010, net worth was lower than it had been in 2001 for most American families, an entire decade lost.

Net worth fell much more steeply than income during the recession, making families relatively more dependent on income than on assets than they were before the recession began. That would be manageable news if income growth had been strong over the period, but it wasn't. The combined effect of plunging net worth, flat or falling income, and high unemployment means that a large number of American families are simply poorer today, at least on paper, than they were six years ago—which has had and will continue to have significant implications for college affordability and accessibility.

Tomorrow Never Knows

In early February 2007, my brother called to tell me that he and his family would be featured in a lead story on the *CBS Evening News*. That sounded ominous; lead stories usually feature political battles, military battles, or courtroom battles—war, arrests, and mayhem. Thankfully, we didn't have to worry about any of those ugly topics. The subject of the story was, however, both uncomfortable and important. My brother's family was part of a feature piece headlined, "Savings at Lowest Rate since Depression,"[18] which highlighted a government report indicating that the US savings rate for 2006 was negative—people had tapped into their savings to support or meet their expenses. Robert Samuelson, economics correspondent for the *Washington Post* and *Newsweek,* noted in the story that people were spending and not saving because the economy was so good. Though his comment was not offered as a prognostication, in less than a year the economy would no longer be so good.

My brother's family was selected by *CBS News* producers to broadly represent American families everywhere. I had to think carefully then about whether it was a good thing or a bad thing that members of my family were chosen as the poster representation of Americans' struggle to save. In the end, though, my sister-in-law likely captured the sentiments and experiences of a large swath of Middle America at the time: "We're not the Rockefellers, but we're doing just fine. I'm surprised by how much money we're making. And I'm constantly asking myself, 'Hey wait a minute, how come we're running out of money at the end of the month?'"

In an ideal world, like the ant in Aesop's fable "The Grasshopper and the Ant," families everywhere would have and take the opportunity to look beyond the pressures and pleasures of today to prepare for the necessities and pleasures of tomorrow. The grueling work of the ant described by Aesop notwithstanding, the basic message is downhome and straightforward: saving for tomorrow is a good and wise thing to do. Unfortunately, the reality of the present as well as consumer behavior in America very often belies that sentiment. Not all families are able to save and invest, and many others who are able choose to forgo the opportunity.

There are a variety of ways to look at saving in America, but all of them yield a similar conclusion: we are a nation of spenders, not savers. Perhaps more accurately, we are a nation of "hopers," not planners. And, unfortunately, hope is not a strategy. After reaching a peak of nearly 12 percent in

1981—when both inflation rates and interest rates were very high—the personal saving rate in the United States (a highly aggregated figure measuring total personal savings in the country as a percentage of total disposable personal income—essentially how much money is left after spending as a percentage of income) trended steadily downward for the next twenty-five years, reaching its dismal bottom in mid-2005 at just over 1 percent.[19] By that point, there was no place to go but up. Similar to what had occurred in prior recessions, the personal savings rate did rise during the Great Recession, peaking at just over 6 percent in late 2008. It has declined since then, but it remains higher than the average for the ten years prior to the recession. That would appear to be at least a glimmer of good news from an overall financial health standpoint.

Unfortunately, the aggregate personal savings rate provides few insights into the actual savings behavior and choices of real families. The Federal Reserve Board's triennial *Survey of Consumer Finances* addresses at least some of those questions by asking families directly whether their spending was less than, more than, or the same as their income in the prior year. Its research offers a more granular and locally based assessment of actual saving behavior. The responses provided by families are not particularly encouraging. Between 1992 and 2007, 55 percent to 60 percent of all families indicated that they saved (that is, their incomes exceeded their spending).[20] However, while the aggregate personal savings rate in the United States increased during the recession, the percentage of families indicating that they saved anything actually dropped to 52 percent by 2010.

The seemingly contradictory claims suggest that families who saved often set aside a lot of money (which would push the value of personal savings up) but that many more saved nothing at all (which would push the rate of savings down). The latter figure—the proportion of the population that actually saves, independent of the amount they save—is just as important to colleges and universities because it provides a broader indication of the general preparedness of families for college expenses. And the results suggest little reason for optimism on that front. Most families are woefully underprepared.

The Federal Reserve survey probes family saving habits, examining how often they set aside money and whether they do it consciously or as little more than a derivate of expenditures not incurred. In 2010, one-quarter of all families reported that they either saved nothing (their income equaled their spending) or that their spending typically exceeded their income. Just over one-third of families said that they saved income not expended at year's end—less a choice than a coincidence. Only 4 in 10 families indicated that they regularly saved money.

The financial vehicles most commonly used by families aren't designed to provide much of a lift to what families are able to save. While more than 90 percent of all American families hold a transactional account, primarily in the form of checking, savings, or money market accounts, fewer than 1 in 6 own any other kind of nonretirement financial asset (like certificates of deposit, savings bonds, stocks, or bonds).[21] Though transaction accounts are among the safest and easiest ways to save and access money, in the low-interest environment that has dominated the financial world since the Great Recession, they typically offer the lowest rates of return, most often not pro-

---

The savings news could not be much worse for colleges and universities. Too many families will face college expenses with woefully inadequate savings. That much is already true. Sallie Mae reported that during the 2012–13 academic year, average contributions from parent college savings funds or other savings and investments supported only 10 percent of the total cost of attendance at four-year colleges and universities in the United States.* Even among the highest-income parents—those with incomes over $100,000—savings supported only an average of 21 percent of tuition, fees, room, board, and expenses. The lack of adequate savings will continue to put enormous pressure on family income and financial aid as sources of support for college expenses, particularly as those expenses rise.

Saving requires not just resources available to be saved but also a habit of saving. By the time children reach college age, saving behaviors are long established. In a conversation about college costs years ago, a family friend whose oldest child was 14 at the time told me that they had not yet begun to think about saving and planning for the costs of their children's college education. I had no sage advice to offer. Game over. For colleges and universities to meaningfully influence saving for higher education, we need to reach out to families much earlier—when their children are very young or in preschool—to provide financial planning advice and assistance, a responsibility we too often now leave to chance.

*Sallie Mae and Ipsos Public Affairs. *How American Pays for College 2013,* April 2014, Table 15a, https://salliemae.newshq.businesswire.com/sites/salliemae.newshq.businesswire.com/files/doc _library/file/Sallie_Mae_Report_-_How_America_Pays_for_College_Report_FINAL_0.pdf. According to the Sallie Mae research, parental savings covered an average of just 7% of total attendance costs at private four-year colleges and 14% of total attendance costs at public four-year colleges (Table 15c).

viding returns that match the rate of inflation. In other words, most families neither have a habit of regular saving nor hold the type of financial assets intended to boost the value of their savings.

It is not simply a matter of whether families save or not. Often, the amounts they indicate having saved or on-hand are shockingly low, at least in relation to the costs they would incur for college or for retirement. According to the Federal Reserve analysis, in 2010 the median value of family checking, savings, and money market accounts in the United States, the most widely held types of financial assets, totaled just $3,500. In a 2012 survey by the Employee Benefit Research Institute, 60 percent of all employed Americans over age 25 reported that the total value of their savings and investments (excluding the value of their homes or defined benefit plans) was below $25,000. Less than one-third reported savings of more than $50,000.[22] Considered in total, Americans are remarkably unprepared for either college or retirement expenses.

Unemployment Drag

No single economic event is more feared than losing a job. Though monthly employment data are reported in aggregated and detached terms, loss of work is a deeply disruptive personal experience, particularly when it occurs against a backdrop of little or no savings, high expenses, and high personal debt (each all too common among American families). Unemployment is a key statistic, not just because of the personal devastation it wreaks and the economic drag it creates, but also because the figure itself, even independent of personal experience, fuels social and political anxiety. It is as important perceptually as it is in reality.

Persistently high unemployment is a nagging remnant of the Great Recession. In mid-2007, the national unemployment rate stood at 4.4 percent. By the end of 2010 it had reached 10 percent, the highest level of joblessness since the early 1980s. While job numbers have improved since then, they have not yet returned to anything close to prerecession levels, mostly staying stuck between 7 percent and 8 percent.[23] By 2013, 1 in 7 Americans—more than 23 million people—remained unemployed, marginally employed, or involuntarily employed part-time.[24] More troubling, those defined as long-term unemployed (out of work for more than twenty-seven weeks) today make up nearly 40 percent of all the unemployed, more than twice historic averages and suggestive of a long-term structural unemployment problem in America.

Unemployment rates have been highest among those with the least education and for black and Hispanic workers.

Not only has unemployment remained high, but the jobs created in the postrecession recovery overwhelmingly have been concentrated in lower-wage occupations, creating a further drag on the economy and over the longer term continuing to limit growth in family income. The data are striking. According to research conducted by the National Employment Law Project in mid-2012, lower-wage occupations—which they defined as jobs paying $28,000 or less annually—accounted for approximately one-fifth of the jobs lost in the recession but have provided nearly 60 percent of the jobs created in the recovery. By comparison, while 60 percent of job losses incurred during the Great Recession were in middle-wage occupations—jobs paying between about $28,000 and $43,000—those same occupations have provided only 22 percent of jobs created since then. Higher-wage occupations, the jobs college graduates and their parents dream about and expect, represent only 20 percent of all postrecession job gains.[25] Clearly, this picture could turn around. More middle-wage and higher-wage jobs could be created as the economy improves and grows. But until that happens, colleges and universities everywhere will have to address the twin issues of high unemployment and the erosion of the economic middle among their students' families.

Weak labor markets and, in particular, high unemployment rates, feed insecurity and uncertainty. Each has implications for students planning for college and colleges planning for students. Almost surely overlooked outside of the financial aid office or the economics department, the changing employment situation and how it influences current and prospective students needs closer attention from colleges and university leaders.

Unemployment trends impact colleges in two key ways. For prospective students with an unemployed parent, or a parent facing the very real prospect of losing a job, college choices—not only where to go to school but even whether to go at all—can be dramatically altered. For current students with a parent who recently lost a job, their ability to stay in school and complete their degree may be threatened, which often requires that their institution provide them with additional financial aid. Perhaps most importantly, persistently high unemployment rates may change the way both prospective and current students perceive the value of their college experience and degree, placing much more emphasis on it as an economically defensive activity than as a developmental activity. Changing values borne of a new economic landscape and new economic realities can have significant implications for the return-on-investment calculus.

Borrowing and Debt

In February 2013, the Federal Reserve Bank of New York released a report indicating that total outstanding student loan balances for all borrowers across the country had approached $1 trillion in 2012, a staggering and eye-catching figure by almost any definition.[26] The data reflected loan balances for those currently in school as well as those no longer enrolled, represent-ing millions of borrowers of all ages and types. The Federal Reserve Bank noted in its report that total outstanding student loan balances had doubled since 2006 and that student debt was the only form of household debt—including credit card debt, auto loans, and home equity borrowing—that did not fall during or after the Great Recession. Several months earlier, The Institute for College Access and Success (TICAS) released its seventh annual report detailing state-by-state average cumulative student loan debt of recent graduates from four-year colleges and universities in the United States. In its report, TICAS noted that among the two-thirds of 2011 baccalaureate gradu-ates who borrowed, average cumulative student loan debt totaled $26,600, the highest average ever in nominal terms.[27] Those reports, not surprisingly, yielded a torrent of media stories—typically focused on the wrenching expe-riences, and often poor choices, of individual borrowers—drawing attention to the rising price of college and the crushing and sometimes ruinous loan burdens that have resulted from it.

After the price of college, no other higher education statistic draws as much public attention or creates as much anguish as increasing levels of stu-dent debt. Reports about rising student borrowing create external down-ward pressure on institutional price and upward pressure on policy action to stem its rising tide. No college or university today can afford to overlook the fear and often anger that wells up in response to reports of rising student loan debt. The harder question is what colleges and universities can do about it. And unfortunately, the data offered up for public consumption typically do not paint a complete enough picture to guide college and university deci-sion making.

The basic facts about student borrowing seem straightforward and clear. Annual student borrowing has increased more or less consistently over the last decade, essentially doubling in total in real terms since the 2001–02 academic year.[28] But that is not the whole story. In its 2012 *Trends in Student Aid* report, the College Board noted that the total volume of loans disbursed to current students in 2011–12 *decreased* by more than 4 percent in real terms from the prior year, the first decline in at least two decades. Moreover, while the amounts students borrow has increased over time, the proportion of bachelor's degree recipients who graduate with debt has changed little in the last decade (approximately 55 percent at public institutions and 65 percent at private institutions). And in inflation-adjusted dollars, the average cumulative amounts borrowed by graduates of public and private not-for-profit institutions rose by less than $4,000 among public college students and by less than $7,000 for private college students between 2001 and 2011—each less than the real change in the average comprehensive price of attendance at those institutions over the same period, meaning that for some students loans financed a smaller, not larger, share of the total multiyear cost of attendance in 2011 than they did in 2001.

None of those figures diminish the reality that some students borrow extraordinary amounts to finance their undergraduate and graduate education. But does it mean that *all* student borrowers risk landing on the precipice of financial calamity? No. While anguished stories about enormous student loan debt make great media copy, those kinds of experiences are not the norm. The Federal Reserve Bank noted in its 2013 report that nearly 70 percent of all outstanding student loan balances in 2012, inclusive of balances for undergraduate as well as graduate students, were below $25,000— and that fewer than 4 percent of those outstanding balances totaled more than $100,000.

Student debt figures are almost always collected and reported as averages, which can cloud consumer and policy understanding of what is really happening in the marketplace. Averages very often are influenced by choices made at the extreme, the highs pulling the average up (or pushing it down). As a result, they may not convey an accurate picture of the real experiences of typical students. At my own institutions, the median amount of cumulative debt at graduation among those who borrowed consistently runs 10 percent less than the average figure we are asked to report publicly, a difference driven by the choices of a small number of students who borrowed very large sums. In our case, the median clearly represents the typical experience of borrowers better than the average. It is important to know and understand the difference.

Student loan default rates—the Armageddon figure of borrowing, since student loan debt cannot be discharged through bankruptcy–also have risen, from under 5 percent among borrowers who entered repayment in 2003 to 9 percent among borrowers who entered repayment in 2010. But even so, they remain well below the 22 percent peak experienced in 1990.[29] In other words, the vast majority of student borrowers manage their debt. Yes, their debt may cause them to make financial trade-offs in their lives, but so do all other spending decisions (and most of those do not offer the long-term economic return of a college degree). Moreover, the incidence of default is not evenly distributed among all types of degree-granting institutions. Students attending for-profit postsecondary institutions made up fewer than 1 in 8 students enrolled in college in the United States in 2008–09 but 28 percent of those who entered repayment the next year and nearly half of those who defaulted on their student loans by September 2010.[30]

Answers to questions about how much students should borrow for college or whether all students should be subject to the same borrowing limits are not at all clear. Unlike most other forms of borrowing, which typically require a physical form of collateral, the only collateral required for most student loans (those not cosigned by parents or someone else) is the student's future prospects. Absent a particularly clear set of standards for student borrowing, or even a clear expectation of the student's economic potential, we are left to judge individual borrowing in mostly subjective terms of good or bad and aggregate borrowing by equally subjective assessments of *ex post* student outcomes and loan default rates.

Unfortunately, it's unlikely that even a best-practice understanding of student lending would position colleges and universities to effectively change levels or rates of student and family borrowing for college. Americans love to borrow. Between 1980 and 2000, outstanding consumer credit, inclusive of revolving and nonrevolving debt, increased by nearly five times, rising from $352 billion to more than $1.7 trillion in nominal terms.[31] That debt financed every consumer product or experience imaginable. Why do we borrow so much? The answer may well be as simple as, because we can. As access to credit in America has expanded over the last forty years, individuals and families across the country have taken full advantage of their expanded purchasing power. The spending generated by consumer borrowing fuels a significant part of the American economy. When capital resources are readily available, wants quickly can become needs, sometimes irrespective of the terms associated with access to those resources. And ill-considered debt-financed spending can rapidly exceed any reasonable future prospects for paying it back. That story played out in often very sad ways throughout the Great Recession.

In the context of the American love affair with debt spending, it is not particularly surprising that students and families today borrow as much as they do to finance their college education. Student loan capital from government and nongovernment sources is widely available and by and large easily accessible. Moreover, the repayment requirements often seem a distant worry rather than a current reality. Irrespective of the price of college, borrowing to pay for college in some ways represents the easiest of money—particularly when interest rates are favorable, no collateral is required, and repayment is years away. In that sense, students may behave exactly like their parents and American consumers in general, responding similarly to a similar set of incentives but with one very important difference from the vantage point of economic development: borrowing for education represents an investment in human capital development rather than an act of consumption-driven spending.

In June 2013, the Congressional Joint Economic Committee Democratic Staff issued a report assessing the causes and consequences of rising student loan debt.[32] Much like other analyses examining the same issue, the Congressional report assessed trends in student borrowing and the consequences associated with rising debt levels and then offered a number of policy prescriptions for consideration. Most notably, the report placed the blame for increased borrowing squarely on the rising price of college, describing it in simple cause-and-effect terms. It is true that the real price of college has increased much faster than the rate of consumer inflation for many years. The inflation-adjusted average comprehensive price of attendance (which includes tuition, fees, room, and board) rose by 66 percent at private colleges and by 110 percent at public colleges between 1994 and 2014.[33] Without doubt, rising college prices have helped fuel rising student borrowing. But that explanation is too neat and simple—correlation and causality are two very different things—and masks a much more difficult and challenging reality for colleges and universities as well as for students and families.

Colleges and universities own the sticker price and the net price they bring to market. They do not, however, control economic cycles or the family financial behavior that influences the market's response to either sticker price or net price. Popular media stories notwithstanding, borrowing deci-

Falling incomes, falling net worth led by falling home values, unstable employment, and poor savings habits—combined with America's wholesale acceptance of debt financing as a means to satisfy current consumption—all have conspired to put enormous pressure on student borrowing independent of the change in college prices and in spite of tremendous increases in grant and scholarship aid in the last decade. Data compiled by the College Board indicate that the average inflation-adjusted net price of college after all grants, scholarships, and tax credits, increased by only 26 percent at public four-year colleges and universities (a price increase driven by loss of state operating appropriations over the same period) and did not change at private institutions between 2004–05 and 2014–15.* The growth in student borrowing simply cannot be understood only in relation to rising college costs. Even if the price of college had gone up at only the rate of consumer inflation, student borrowing in recent years surely would have increased anyway. Economic circumstances in most American families would have demanded it.

*The College Board Advocacy and Policy Center, *Trends in College Pricing, 2014,* October 2014, https://secure-media.collegeboard.org/digitalServices/misc/trends/2014-trends-college-pricing -report-final.pdf.

sions often occur because of circumstances or choices outside the bounds of institutional control or influence. That makes generating a cogent response to rising student debt particularly challenging.

But challenging or not, rising student loan debt requires the full attention of college leaders. In framing either a financial aid response or a public position, we need to keep a couple of key points in mind. First, student borrowing is here to stay. As long as debt capital for education is readily available to students and families, many will take full advantage of it irrespective of the sticker or net price of college or changes to that price. While some students and families clearly are debt averse (not everyone borrows or wants to borrow), American consumers have for decades taken advantage of their expanding access to debt and there is no reason to believe they will act differently in relation to access to education debt.

More importantly, borrowing for education can only be understood in terms of its investment value and not simply as a current consumption expenditure. At its simplest, student borrowing represents a bet on the future— for many borrowers, a true act of optimism. It reflects an investment in personal development and potential, economic and social. Venture capitalists place similar bets on start-up enterprises every day. Colleges and universities must describe student loan borrowing in compelling investment terms, which in turn requires them to understand and then express something about the real return to the investment.

Mostly through its silence on the issue, higher education collectively has ceded far too much ground to the increasingly popular position that all student borrowing is bad borrowing. It isn't. Nor do all college students borrow extraordinary sums; most don't. The only way to understand the value of student debt is to understand the investment return. Not only do institutions need to think that way, they also need to help students and families to think that way.

The decision about how much to borrow for college ultimately rests with students and families. Some borrowing decisions indeed are poor decisions, and colleges need to guide students and their families as best they can to avoid those choices—even if it means recommending that continued enrollment at their institution is no longer the best option. For others, the ability to borrow provides access to a world of opportunity not otherwise available. The distinction is important, both for students and for colleges and universities.

The March of Economic Evolution

What made the Great Recession so disruptive at the time, and a continuing source of disruption today, was its scale and ferocity. Almost no one was left untouched. The economic havoc it wrought continues to influence families years later, both in real and perceptual ways. The Great Recession exposed the extraordinary fragility of family balance sheets, diminishing their ability to comfortably or even adequately finance a college education for their children.

It just as often exposed the fragility of our own institutional operations. Family incomes had been stagnant or declining (in real terms) for years prior to the recession. And the pre–financial aid price of college in relation to income was rising long before the downturn began. The recession significantly accelerated the income decline, reducing the purchasing power of income in relation to the still rising price of college. At the same time, it badly damaged net worth. In a culture that has neither the habit nor the inclination to save regularly, the reductions in net worth knocked out one of the foundation assumptions of college financial planning—the availability of past resources earned from assets, savings, and investments to help pay for college. Falling or flat family income, combined with diminished net worth and inadequate savings, has put substantially more pressure on borrowing as a tool for students to pay college expenses and on institutional and government investments in student financial aid. Nothing in the postrecession economic environment suggests any change to those fundamental conditions or pressures.

Most colleges and universities will not have the ability to consistently and significantly raise revenue from the net tuition paid by students and families at a rate sufficient to cover the costs of education anytime soon. The combined effects of slow postrecession economic growth and the changing demographic characteristics of the rising traditional-age college population suggest that scarcity and uncertainty will remain the signature economic themes for the foreseeable future. How colleges and universities individually and collectively address those issues will make all the difference in the world to affordability, accessibility, and the quality of the learning experiences we provide.

We also need to take a deep breath. Economic cycles come and go. Though we often fool ourselves into thinking that "this time will be different," the march of economic evolution has never played out in an indefinitely straight line, up or down. The ugly details of the recession and its wide wake are not meant to suggest that bleakness and long-term despair have become our lot. They have not, unless we choose that path. But it is only in understanding how the economic disruption has influenced our prospective students, our current students, and our institutional operations that we can position ourselves to take on the challenges the disruption poses. We do not control any of the economic or demographic forces of disruption but are subject to them. And for that reason, we can neither ignore them nor wish them away. Their effects will influence our financial aid practice and choices as well as our budget practices and choices for years to come. Our responsibility as leaders demands, first, understanding and then action.

CHAPTER FIVE

Cultural Disruption

It is not so very important for a person to learn facts. For that, he does not really need a college. He can learn them from books. The value of an education in a liberal arts college is not learning of many facts but the training of the mind to think something that cannot be learned from textbooks.

—Albert Einstein

Two other forces of disruption—one long-developing, the other emerging—also exert significant influence on our present and future: the commoditization of higher education and the continuing evolution of technologically aided mass-market higher education. Though derived in part from economic and demographic disruption, these forces reflect cultural and technological changes that strike at the heart of historic educational values and practices at many colleges and universities. They very often test our institutional purposes, the values that have shaped them, and the ways we express them. Though these forces ought not to be described or interpreted in wholly negative terms, they present many institutions with uncomfortable and difficult choices.

At their core, the commodity narrative of higher education and the technological massification of higher education suggest that efficiency and simplicity are or ought to be transcendent values in the provision of college. Straight lines from point A to point B. Simple, easy-to-understand objectives. Clear pathways. Less cost (presumably). Straightforward business values applied to higher education.

Efficiency and simplicity surely are worthy operational objectives. On balance, people prefer Occam's razor to Rube Goldberg. College and university leaders do, too, and we ought to resist the implied antonym, wastefulness. However, efficiency and simplicity do not come without a price or absent the need for trade-offs. They must be considered in the context of the values institutions hold, the objectives we seek, and the educational practices that form the core of our experiences. And on those fronts, many colleges and universities today clearly are fighting an uphill battle.

The Changing Collegiate Context

Before exploring the forces of cultural and technological disruption now pressing on much of higher education, it is worth taking a moment to consider the context in which a college education occurs. Changes in the factors that shape and define the college experience have provided fuel to the disruption. The basic college experience consists of two independent but ultimately interactive and interdependent parts, one uniquely owned by students, the other by colleges and universities themselves. The framework can be simply conveyed in the form of an easy-to-remember schematic.

Students (and these days very often their parents) bring three things to the table when they enroll in college: their aptitude, their motivation, and their aspirations. They own those values and attributes. Each is shaped in a variety of ways long before they ever show up on our campuses or in our classrooms. Aptitude, motivation, and aspiration all are influenced by the environments in which our students live and grow up—in their families, in their schools, with their friends, and by the broader culture. Colleges can influence but never own all three. That's an important point. On the one hand,

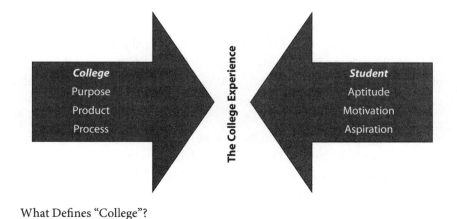

What Defines "College"?

we take students as they come to us, each one a unique bundle of values and characteristics. On the other, their values and attributes act on us, shaping and reshaping our own institutional values and practices.

Colleges and universities also bring three distinct features to the educational table: our purpose (embodied in our mission and values), our product (the constellation of courses and experiences we provide to our students), and our processes (the ways we deliver the experiences we provide). Together, those values and attributes represent not only what we offer to our students but what we pledge to society at large. Similar to the values and attributes of our students, our institutional purposes, products, and processes are drawn from our history, our values, and the changing needs and demands of the world around us. Because they typically have been shaped over many decades, we often hold them very dear—resisting the temptation to faddish change, and sometimes to any change at all.

The successful fulfillment of our students' aspirations requires their full commitment and effort. Students do not simply receive their education, they give it form and define its outcomes. This is true at every level of schooling. A course can be magnificently constructed and brilliantly presented, but without the active engagement of the student's aptitude, motivation, and aspiration, little learning or development will occur. The bargain, of course, works in reverse, too. Bright, fully engaged students get little out of college experiences that are poorly constructed or poorly presented. In either case, no input yields no outcome. By definition and necessity, education is an interactive process, an exchange, colleges and their students acting on each other.

The engagement of a student's aptitude, motivation, and aspirations with an institution's purpose, product, and processes comprises the touchstone of the collegiate experience. When those values and attributes are reasonably well aligned (what we would describe in simpler terms as a good *fit*), the educational experience yields marvelous results: engaged students who identify with the values of our institutions and take full advantage of the range of learning opportunities we provide to create powerful developmental outcomes. A happy ending for everyone.

When they are not well aligned, it is a different and more complicated story. The sum total of the abilities, motivation, and aspirations of our students represent our market. They collectively define what is desired and valued. When marketplace values and objectives do not align well with our own purposes, product, or processes, we face considerably more difficult educational and operational choices. What we believe is essential and what the market believes is essential don't match. In a state of disequilibrium, some-thing has to give. Most often it is us—our culture, our values, and our practices—and not the marketplace that must adapt under the new rules of the game. Today, the values that define the culture of many institutions in-creasingly are out of sync with the evolving cultural values and expectations of the marketplace.

Higher Education as Commodity

Com•mod•i•ty. (1) A mass-produced unspecialized good. (2) Something useful or valued. (3) A good or service whose wide availability typically leads to smaller profit margins and diminishes the importance of factors (such as brand name) other than price.[1]

———————

The term "commodity" typically is used in a consumer context to describe products like bread or toothpaste—ubiquitous, mass-produced necessities that, in spite of the seeming number of choices and the power of advertising to create differences and preferences, are nearly indistinguishable from each other. Most who work in higher education would resist as both distasteful and inappropriate the notion that a college education is similar to a con-sumer commodity. We understand the significance of what we do from the ground level, and have (or profess to have) a granular and meaningful sense of the distinctive value provided at our institutions. We do not see sameness, nor even mass production. We also do not typically view the singular, or even central, purpose of higher education as the production of a credential.

And yet, protestations notwithstanding, American higher education today seems to share many of the characteristics of common consumer commodities. Colleges and universities as a group often behave like other commodity-producing industries. Clearly what higher education does is valued—the steadily rising demand for college and high college participation rates alone indicate as much. At the same time, though, it would be difficult to reject the assertion that postsecondary education today is mass produced, or at least provided en masse. The thousands of colleges in the United States each year enroll millions of students. And the experience increasingly is less location bound, available digitally to anyone, anywhere, and at any time. While the education each student receives may be different or personal, the totality of the experience was long ago brought to scale to serve very large numbers of people.

Even the academic programs offered by colleges and universities, considered across all institutions, often have something of a commodity feel from the vantage point of prospective students. A quick perusal of the more than 2,700 institutions offering bachelor's degrees who are included in the popular *Peterson's Guide* indicates that nearly 1,700 offer degrees in psychology, more than 1,500 in biology or history, and nearly 1,200 in economics, just to name a few.[2] While any individual institution must understand the distinctiveness of its own academic programs and its own faculty, it has not been my experience that the typical prospective college student and her or his parents are either so well informed or so discerning. What we understand on campus as differentiation or specialization at our institution is not nearly as clear to prospective students during their college search. We see distinction; they see thousands of similarly described psychology, biology, history, or economics programs. Little about the way we go to market—on our websites, in our printed publications, or even in the classroom visits we arrange— makes it easier for most prospective students or their parents to meaningfully or more than superficially discern academic differences, either in departmental majors or among core curricula.

It is difficult to stand out in a crowded marketplace offering an indistinguishable product, experience, or outcome. Lacking an historic, strong, or differentiated brand position, many organizations, including colleges and universities, turn to the most powerful and efficient market tool they have to

As higher education has expanded, reaching more people with more programs than ever before, it has become less discretely distinguishable, particularly as institutions of all types use similar language and images to describe who they are and what they do. The number of colleges and universities who can legitimately lay claim to a strong and distinctive brand position (institutions like those in the Ivy League, for example) never has been large. On the whole, colleges and universities most often look and act more alike than unalike. As my oldest son began his college search process, I was struck by the sameness of the early mail we received: nearly identical letters making nearly identical claims and offering nearly identical "rewards" for returning an enclosed mailer (many to be returned, oddly enough, to the same mail house in Ohio). Nothing in those early pitch pieces set one college apart from the other, a particular complication when more than one search piece arrived on the same day.

reach their goals: price manipulation.[3] A college can induce demand for an undifferentiated product by effectively manipulating its price. And today many institutions do just that across a very wide range of students, which helps to explain why tuition discounting (the accounting term for financial aid spending) is rising and will continue to rise. Effectively employed, differentiated pricing strategies can help institutions reach both their enrollment and net revenue goals. However, a poorly employed race-to-the-bottom pricing strategy comes with its own price—limited (or sometimes nonexistent) growth in revenue from tuition and difficulty managing retention as half-interested students seeking the best price deal learn that perhaps they did not choose very well. When price itself becomes the commodity, quality and experience often will suffer.

Rankings, Rankings Everywhere

About a dozen years ago, I asked a college president I liked and admired what he thought of his institution's placement in the *US News* rankings of colleges and universities. He said he never thought about it. I didn't believe it for a minute.

We live in a culture that loves ranked lists. We rate everything from cars, toasters, and fruit drinks to hospitals, lawyers, and colleges. More importantly, we love winners—those at the top of lists. Recall Nike's advertisement during the 1996 Atlanta Olympics: "You Don't Win Silver, You Lose Gold." While the ad was widely criticized at the time for its vaguely unsportsmanlike and competitively unhealthy tone, it almost certainly captured our cultural fascination with finishing on top. And Nike surely knew it. This is not a new phenomenon. The first issue of *Consumer's Union Reports* (the predecessor to today's *Consumer Reports*) appeared in 1936, complete with reviews of milk, cereal, and soap. The *Guinness Book of World Records* was first published in 1955 and became an immediate bestseller. The 1977 *Book of Lists* was a bestseller through multiple reprints and editions for more than a decade.

Higher education is not independent of the culture that surrounds it. Colleges and universities like lists, too. And, in spite of complaints each year when college rankings are released, most not only like being on those lists, they also like being on top of the lists–at least the good lists. They can validate our sense of self, or at other times offend it. *US News and World Report* published its first "America's Best Colleges" ranking in 1983 (it became an annual report beginning in 1985). If readership numbers are an indicator of success, it was a brilliant idea—and one that has shaped the higher education ranking game for the last twenty-five years. The success of the *US News* rankings has spawned an industry of "me too" rankings, including *Forbes, Money, Time, Newsweek, Kiplinger's, Princeton Review,* and *Washington Monthly,* among others. Even *Cosmopolitan* magazine got into the game for a while. Each is trying to capture some audience's attention to build readership and contribute to the bottom line. None measures or values exactly the same thing. And colleges and universities most often willingly provide the data that sustains nearly all of them.

Love them or hate them, rankings and "best of" lists are here to stay. The genie will not return to the bottle any time soon. They have become important to the college choice process because they seem to provide information objectively, they feature data that are easily counted and measured (even if not well understood), and they purport to condense and convey otherwise complicated or undifferentiated information. They also capture a basic human need for order. Do they oversimplify? Certainly. Do they suggest an inappropriate or meaningless level of precision? Absolutely. Do they distill a wide array of data into something people find simpler to understand and consider? Without a doubt. Rankings and lists are the ultimate sound bites in a sound bite culture. And higher education's own desire to flood the marketplace with competing and too often vague claims provides fertile ground for their creation and consumption.

Unfortunately, the more-popular-than-ever college ranking cottage industry most often does not help to create distinction and may actually worsen commodity pressures. All ranked lists anchor the standard for "best" across only a limited range of criteria and in relation to the top-scoring institutions—creating a force for emulation that can diminish, rather than enhance, institutional distinctiveness.[4] The too common result is that colleges rush to copy, which leads to a kind of referential sameness in the marketplace that makes it harder for anyone to understand the difference between you and me. Each of us is actively working to behave and look just like the other—creating a kind of marketplace tautology. The most effective way for me to rise in a group of ranked institutions is to seek to perform the same as or better than the institutions who are positioned ahead of me. Not to be different, only better in relation to a handful of fixed criteria. Better is no easy task, but different is even more difficult and risky in a market that values and rewards a singular best.

Are Harvard, Princeton, Amherst, or Williams the best colleges in the country (they are according to some rankings)? For some students, the answer undoubtedly is yes, but for others—including many very good students—it is no. If we live in a world that defines success by a singular champion, then everyone else can only lose. After all, you don't win silver, you lose gold. Rather than turning rankings and "best of" lists into a winner-takes-all quest built on unachievable emulation, it would be preferable for colleges and universities to present the lists selectively as tools to help students understand and sort what is most important and least important about what they do and don't do. That surely will create more winners in the process and perhaps even help define a position of distinction in an otherwise commoditized marketplace.

The Transcendence of the Transactional Narrative

Fueled by economic and social change, over the last sixty years higher education has evolved from a luxury good to a necessity good, a *sine qua non* experience for access to the American middle class. The rising (and now substantial) economic return to a college degree, the labor market's demand for more highly educated workers, and the growing number of people who pursue a college education each has contributed to an ascending commodity narrative for higher education—the desire to express the value of the collegiate experience in primarily instrumental or transactional terms rather than in developmental terms.

Today parents and policy makers alike typically describe their expectations for higher education economically and judge its performance in relation to expected economic outcomes. Research by both Sallie Mae and Public Agenda on how Americans view college is telling. In 2012, more than 7 in 10 current college students and their parents strongly agreed that going to college was important because a college degree was required for their (or their child's) desired occupation. A similar percentage said they attended college because they believed they would earn more money after obtaining a college degree.[5] Those views are broadly shared by the public at large. More than half of all Americans today believe that a college education is necessary to succeed in the work world, up from just 31 percent in 2000.[6] Nearly half also believe that the primary purpose of college is to teach specific skills and knowledge that can be used in the workplace.[7]

College students get that message loud and clear. In fall 2014, nearly 9 in 10 first-time new entering students at four-year colleges and universities nationally indicated that the ability to get a better job was a very important factor influencing their decision to go to college. Three-quarters also identified training for a specific career as very important.[8] Job, career, and money concerns have for many years been cited as key reasons for going to college.

Those impressions should hardly come as a surprise in difficult economic times. A college degree offers a form of economic security or opportunity no longer widely available to those who do not pursue postsecondary education of some kind. The earnings premium for those with a baccalaureate degree widened during the 1990s and remained wide during and after the recession.[9] College graduates also are much more likely to be employed than those who do not have a college degree; in early 2013, the national unemployment rate for those with a bachelor's degree or higher was under 4 percent, compared to nearly 8 percent for those with only a high school diploma.[10]

All of these data suggest that college has passed the economically important to economically necessary Rubicon. That certainly is the way prospective students and their families see it today. Going to college and completing a degree promises access to a potential economic pot of gold (never mind that effort, ability, career choices, and luck play an enormous role in any individual's experience). For their part, colleges and universities everywhere have for decades advanced, ridden, and capitalized on the trend to rising economic returns to education.

The ascending and now dominant instrumental or commodity narrative of the college experience poses two significant challenges to many institutions, one related to expectations of return on investment and the other related to competing educational values and objectives.

ROI

Though the economic returns to education become particularly important during hard times, does a college degree guarantee economic success? Emphatically, no. To paraphrase any investment prospectus, individual results do in fact vary, often significantly. Few colleges would dare get into the business of guaranteeing or even appearing to guarantee successful employment or income outcomes for their graduates. An institution's role is preparatory and, in any case, larger than simply preparing students for particular jobs or career tracks that exist today. More importantly, colleges do not control labor markets or broad economic trends, though we contribute to and are subject to both. Consider employment prospects. The national unemployment rate in fall 2006 was just 4.4 percent (the unemployment rate for college graduates then was under 2%!).[11] The unemployment rate had fallen more or less consistently since 1992—meaning it had trended downward for most of the lives of the traditional-age students who entered college as bright-eyed first-year students that fall. If past performance were any indicator of future performance, everything looked wonderful. But it wasn't. By the time the entering class of 2006 graduated four years later, the unemployment rate had more than doubled, rising to 9.5 percent, making postcollege employment prospects considerably more difficult. And leaving people to wonder about the promise of college.

Were colleges to blame for a bad economy? No. Does a bad economy change the way people view the college experience, particularly given the importance they place on the economic outcomes they expect? Likely. Students and their families are legitimately concerned about what awaits them at the end of the education rainbow. The cost of making a "wrong" decision—choosing the wrong institution or the wrong academic major—appears very high. The coupling effect of rising college costs and seemingly diminished economic returns makes colleges and universities particularly vulnerable to the effects of the commodity narrative. What we provide—a degree—is nearly universally lionized as necessary to economic sustainability and success. But when we fall short of delivering on that promise or hope, we often are demonized as ineffective, inefficient, and sometimes even corrupt.

All institutions must provide convincing (and research-based) answers to the following questions often asked by prospective students, their families, and even policy makers: What are the employment (or volunteer or graduate school) experiences of your recent graduates? How have those changed over time? What kinds of jobs and career experiences do your graduates have? What kinds of incomes do they earn (not just the grand average)? How

> Colleges and universities are adept at using soaring rhetorical verse to describe their learning communities and their commitment to excellence. They typically are equally adept at reciting the facts that comprise their experience: the number of majors, student-to-faculty ratios, class sizes, and perhaps even the volume of library holdings. But students and families have two abiding concerns today as they consider college and their investment in it: can we afford this institution, and what kind of return can we expect at the end of this experience? More simply, will I get what I pay for?

effective is your institution in preparing students for employment or graduate school and providing them with access to employment and postbaccalaureate opportunities?

College and university leaders can talk about learning value to their heart's content, but if we cannot address economic concerns in a compelling way—which does not require promises or guarantees but does require a commitment to understanding what happens to our students after they graduate—we risk losing the argument altogether. Parents are particularly interested in our answers, fearing their worst-imagined outcome will come true: their son or daughter will come home from college without prospects to live in their basement, eat their food, and watch reruns of *The Big Bang Theory*. A result for which they will hold us accountable. Families and policy makers care deeply about these issues. So, then, should everyone on campus, trustees, administrators, faculty, and staff alike.

Learning Values

In a 2011 survey by the Pew Research Center, more than 8 in 10 college graduates in the country described their postsecondary experience as a good investment.[12] Fully two-thirds of them said their collegiate experience was very useful in helping them to grow and develop as a person, and nearly three-quarters said college was very useful in helping them to develop intellectually. That's the good news.

On the other side of the coin, though, fewer than 4 in 10 Americans (including those who do not have a college degree) believed that the primary purpose of college should be to help an individual grow personally and intellectually. And only 5 percent said that students today receive an excellent value for the money their families spend on college, a devastatingly low number. College graduates and nongraduates responded similarly. Sadly, that sentiment does not appear wholly out of step with higher education's own view of itself. Only 17 percent of all college presidents surveyed at the same time by the Pew Research Center rated the value of higher education today as excellent in relation to what families spend. Clearly we have a serious value problem—both conveying our value and describing our values.

The instrumental narrative of higher education focuses principally on the transactional value of the experience, most often expressed in the form of degree completion or certification as a means to an economic end. The educational narrative embraced by most four-year colleges and universities, on the other hand, focuses on the transformational value of the collegiate experience, its intellectual and developmental utility. The transformational narrative emphasizes a number of key learning outcomes, which typically include personal developmental growth and maturation, the formation and development of habits of the mind, and the development of perspective. While the two narrative frameworks need not be inherently at odds, the ascendance of the instrumental narrative has diminished the strength of the developmental or transformational narrative. While I suspect few students or families would argue with learning and developmental values as at least nice to have, the conversation about higher education today more often suggests that each takes a back seat to the steps required to gain the credential and the ability of the credential to generate an economic return.

A friend of mine years ago described her collegiate aspiration as follows: you go to college to get a job so you can have a life. Though neither a particularly inspiring aspiration nor a representation of all college students' attitudes, that sentiment surely has been held by many students and their parents for a very long time. However, the transactional narrative opens the door to a number of uncomfortable and, for many institutions, untenable conclusions and value conflicts. It positions the economically motivated credential value of the collegiate experience as its primary objective. The act of going to college and earning a degree trumps whatever personal or intellectual development that may occur during the process of earning the degree. I want to be an accountant. Why do I have to take courses in history or English, too? Why does it matter that I live in a residence hall on campus? What difference does it make that I get involved in activities on campus? These are not atypical or out-of-the-box questions. They ought to press us to provide compelling responses demonstrating that our learning values are more than experiential amenities or developmental accessories.

The transactional narrative also suggests that where students go to college matters less than that they acquire a degree somewhere in some way. If the product itself—the experience called higher education in this case—is not well differentiated, and if its outcomes and values are not particularly clear or well understood, then it makes perfect economic sense to pursue the easiest or most direct route to the end at the lowest cost. The credential is what matters, not the place at which it is earned or even how it is earned. The end matters more than the means. Few colleges, of course, believe this about themselves or want to believe it about the marketplace. And not all students engage their college search or their undergraduate experience in this way.

But after conversations with students and families over many years, I am convinced many surely do. The transactional narrative of higher education ultimately threatens to reduce the collegiate experience to little more than a set of linear content hoops through which students must jump—a conclusion directly at odds with the learning values many institutions hold dear.

It also threatens to reduce the value of the collegiate experience to that which can be most easily counted, like the number of degrees conferred. Though easily measured and understood, degree attainment rates ultimately reveal little more than output production. They provide no insights about the quality of the education students receive or whether they left college prepared for work and life. I do not disagree with the institutional or public policy value (even imperative) of pursuing higher rates of degree attainment. But the emphasis on successful degree attainment ought to be wrapped in more than a transactional veneer of "how many." We must also consider larger questions of how to effectively educate students for success. How do we help prospective students make choices that best suit their abilities and aspirations? How do we ensure that the experiences they receive in college provide value that lasts throughout the course of a career or over a lifetime? What values beyond those that we define as economic are important not only to individuals but also to communities and to the nation? These are important questions, the kinds of questions that shape the value narrative of higher education. We ought not to lose sight of them in our zeal to count.

Deus ex Machina

Books will soon be obsolete in the public schools. Scholars will be instructed through the eye. It is possible to teach every branch of human knowledge with the motion picture. Our school system will be completely changed inside of ten years.
—Thomas Edison[13]

I landed a job in the president's office at Saint John's University, my alma mater, after graduating in 1984. In addition to having a real office and a small staff, I was provided with a desktop computer. Personal computers were relatively new then and something of a novelty on campus. Mine was made by IBM. It had a very large green CRT monitor, took up enough space to necessitate a credenza of its own, and required big and fragile floppy disks to run software and save files. My computer offered 64K of memory, a laughably small number in today's terabyte world. Though it was slow and cumbersome to use, it was fascinating and amazing and opened the door to a world of possibility. And today my machine likely rests comfortably somewhere in a Smithsonian museum as an archeological relic from more primitive times.

Fast forward thirty years. Most of the first-year students enrolled at my institutions last year were born in the mid-1990s. Nearly all of them brought their own (very powerful) computers and tablets and smart phones to campus. They have never known anything but instant electronic access to everything and everyone. Their entire world is digitized. My own children are part of this generation and believe their parents were born in the Stone Age. I recently asked one of my sons why he didn't simply telephone his friends to make arrangements to go somewhere, instead of sending them a steady stream of text messages that his fingers seem to manage like a fine pianist. He replied incredulously and with a roll of his eyes, "Dad, you just don't get it." Alas, I have reached *that* age. He and his friends would never understand my generation's awe of Atari Pong.

Technological evolution has always acted as a force of disruption in higher education, shaping and changing the learning experience since long before the advent of computers. The printing press may have been the singularly most important educational innovation in history. Technological development consistently has expanded and democratized access to data and knowledge, as well as access to people. It has removed barriers of time and space in ways that were once unimaginable. And, while colleges often are caricatured as places where pedagogy has stood still for hundreds of years, impervious to changing times, nothing could be further from the truth. Technological innovation not only has changed access to knowledge but also has transformed the tools of discovery. Irrespective of the academic discipline, prospective students today would be hard-pressed to find a course not influenced and shaped by sophisticated tools of technology. It is easy to laugh off Edison's 1913 prediction as a flight of fancy, but the spirit of his statement surely has come to pass (though it took a century rather than a decade).

Technological advancement has enabled the massification of higher education—democratizing access to once closely held knowledge and, ultimately, to college itself in ways previously unimaginable. Today, when people talk about the influence of technology on higher education, they most often mean instruction offered online, either synchronously or asynchronously. While the conversations often engender deep feeling, questions about the value and relevance of online education, in many ways, have already been answered. Online learning clearly has developed more than a toehold as an alternative to traditional classroom instruction. It has become an important part of the nation's composite educational portfolio. In 2011, more than 6.7 million college students—equal to approximately one-third of all students enrolled in postsecondary education—took at least one course online.[14] Though the rate of growth in online course taking has slowed in recent years, the number of students taking an online course has more than doubled since 2005. Today, nearly 9 in 10 institutions of higher education offer at least some form of online coursework or programs, and 7 in 10 indicate that online education is an important component of their long-term institutional strategy. *US News* now ranks "Best Online Programs," a list that in 2013 included baccalaureate programs from institutions as varied as Pace University, Central Michigan University, the University of Florida, and the University of Denver, among many others.[15] Some institutions have expanded the reach of online education through what may best be described as relationships with nontraditional education partners. In spring 2013, for example, Arizona State University announced a financial partnership with Starbucks to provide online education to Starbucks' employees.[16] The rapid development and expansion of online education surely is not a passing fad.

Harvard University's Clayton Christensen has written extensively on the impact of disruptive innovation on traditional industries, including higher education.[17] He defines a disruptive innovation as a product or service that would not meet current standards of "best" but one that is more affordable, easier to use, and ultimately more accessible than the traditional standard. The gestation period for a disruptive innovation may be very long, but its impact can reshape markets, products and services, and production processes. Technological change very often—though not always—serves as a catalyst or enabler for disruption, a kind of prime mover that manifests itself over time as a form of the "creative destruction" described by economist Joseph Schumpeter more than half a century ago.[18]

Christensen cites online learning as a prime example of a disruptive innovation, not as a perfect substitute for traditional learning but rather as a kind of below-the-traditional-production-curve change that over time will (or could) develop further and broaden its appeal. And, in the end, threaten the legacy model of higher education. The idea is both provocative and frightening, as well as too easy to dismiss out of hand by traditional higher education: "online education could never replace the value of what we have successfully provided for hundreds of years." Perhaps that sentiment would be true if one-to-one replacement were the objective or purpose of online learning. But most often it isn't. From a market standpoint, it is more akin to the sacrifice of satisfying in favor of satisficing, a subtle but important difference that in the parlance of economics and market behavior makes all the difference in the world.

The development and proliferation of the Internet by the mid-1990s provided educational opportunities not available before to reach vast new audiences and eliminate barriers of time and geography. Whether online education rises to a position of pedagogical ascendance remains to be seen, as does its long-term impact on the traditional higher education financial model. But we can be certain that its development and proliferation will continue to evolve. The genie is out of the bottle, and few (perhaps no) colleges and universities will be able to ignore or escape its impact.

Of MOOCs and More

Given the rise of online education as an accepted and even widespread practice, it should have come as no great surprise that the latest development, massively open online courses, or MOOCs, would draw so much attention. MOOCs offer full courses online, complete with video lectures and class assignments. They can reach people in every corner of the world at any time. Many today are provided through university consortia (like edX or MITx) or through independent organizations (like Udacity, Coursera, and Kahn Academy). College-affiliated or not, these organizations share the ability to transmit courses and course materials to massive numbers of people, often to hundreds of thousands at a time, at little or no cost on a per-unit basis—a scale that nearly defies imagination. The combination of immense scale and (for now) low market price presents an extraordinary market opportunity for enterprising capitalists and has made MOOCs an object of great interest and popular conversation.

But are we on the cusp of a pedagogical revolution, an evolutionary change in the practice and promise of higher education? The short-term answer is that we don't yet know. The MOOC conversation typically divides higher education professionals (faculty and administrators alike) into two camps: the committed supporters who believe it signals the end of institutional higher education as we know it and the almost Mencken-like skeptics who reject it at every turn as the dereliction of higher education. Like Republicans and Democrats, I suppose, only less entertaining.

Though massive online education is sometimes portrayed as an obvious replacement or fix for traditional higher education, it is not yet clear how the various players creating and offering MOOCs will evolve, what new players will emerge, or whether the application of the technology will yield consistent and sustainable results. Colleges and universities will need to think carefully about whether or how much online learning can effectively replace more traditional classroom learning and for whom. Online learning may work better for some students than others or for some courses better than others. MOOCs clearly offer an efficient means for conveying information and course content to huge numbers of people simultaneously at little cost. But at what price if they eliminate meaningful student-to-student or faculty-to-student dialogue and engagement or do not produce any gains in successful degree completion?

If they continue to evolve as a largely one-way transmittal of information and knowledge, which would seem to be a requirement given their scale, MOOCs will represent the ultimate transactional experience in higher education. A giver and a receiver, mediated by the electronic ether. Colleges and universities worried about the proliferation of massive online learning will have to make, prove, and sustain the claim that education is about more than the conveyance of course content. If higher learning is best practiced as a closely held, personal, and even intimate experience, how much value does the experience add and how much is it worth paying for? New models and new paradigms always force those kinds of questions, and they demand a compelling response.

The economics of the MOOC model are not yet secure, either. Though most of the courses have thus far been offered without charge, they are not free in either an economic or an accounting sense. Someone must ultimately pay for the faculty's expertise, knowledge, and time. Stanford University economist Caroline Hoxby succinctly described the economic uncertainty that swirls around MOOCs:

> It is not clear whether there is a price at which MOOC content is cheap enough to be safe from underselling yet expensive enough to cover the costs of creating and hosting the content. The answer depends on the demand and supply functions about which we currently know next to nothing. The lack of clarity is not only due to the infancy of the MOOC movement (which makes it hard to estimate demand) but also to the current well-intentioned but ultimately confusing tendency of postsecondary institutions to give content to MOOCs for free (making it impossible to estimate supply).[19]

Massive online education does not and surely never will represent a *pro bono* contribution from the professoriate. Who will bear those costs going forward, and how much they will pay, remains to be seen, though it is reasonable to speculate that, as the money-making potential of these courses becomes clearer, more costs will be passed off to its consumers in the form of per-course charges.

The Digital Future

Traditional higher education ignores or wishes away technological forces of disruption at its own peril. Though still facing many questions and challenges, the MOOC movement—if it can be called that at all—has already passed a significant threshold test for market legitimacy. Many of the new cooperatives offering massive online courses were given birth within the halls of the most elite public and private universities in the world—institutions like MIT, the University of California at Berkeley, Stanford, Harvard, and the University of Michigan, among many others. In that sense, the active partnership and advocacy of these extraordinary institutions and their faculty likely has created something of a tipping point favoring the continued development and evolution of vast massive online learning. The economic proposition and juxtaposition seems irresistible: free access to otherwise very costly and, for many, inaccessible higher education. An attractive proposition, indeed.

Up to now, most of the MOOC cooperatives have presented themselves as complements to traditional higher education. The cooperatives do not themselves yet offer formal degrees, and few of them so far offer their courses for credit. However, it is worth asking whether we are trending toward legitimate substitutes for traditional higher education, if not for the whole market, then at least for a growing segment of it. It is not at all difficult to imagine. And even if MOOCs do not evolve as true substitutes for the traditional college experience, what does the advent of broadly available and (for now) less expensive complementary online education mean to traditional institutional practice and degree requirements? Are they a threat to the programs currently offered in the form of displacement of curricula, or a programmatic opportunity in the form of curricular enhancement? Do they offer new opportunities for educational partnerships? None of these choices are mutually exclusive, but they will become increasingly real for institutions looking forward, particularly as economic forces press on colleges and universities from all sides.

Looking beyond MOOCs at the future of online education generally, it is hard to imagine a scenario where it becomes less important. The rising cost of the traditional college experience—reflected in rising prices for students and rising expenses for colleges and universities—will fuel demand for more online education. More students will pursue lower-priced online education, and more institutions will seek to provide it (both as a way to manage costs and to attract new markets or build market share). That it may not provide as many benefits as a traditional educational experience may not matter if the most highly valued end result is transactional rather than developmental. That threat is very real.

The next several years promise fascinating change and experimentation. We don't yet know how it will play out or who will win and who will lose, but college and university leaders do need to pay close attention. Even if we individually choose to stay the current course, we can be assured that the world around us will continue to change.

CHAPTER SIX

No Line on the Horizon

I saw a man pursuing the horizon;
Round and round they sped.
I was disturbed at this;
I accosted the man.
"It is futile," I said,
"You can never—"

"You lie," he cried,
And ran on.
— Stephen B. Crane

Most of the disruptive demographic, economic, and cultural forces reshaping the marketplace and the world of higher education are out of our direct institutional control. They have roots and pathways that live well beyond the limits of our management practice and leadership reach. Still, we are and always have been subject to each of them and their interactive effects.

Prognostication often is a dangerous business if for no other reason than that unexpected events—like the deepest economic downturn since the Great Depression—can intervene to ruin even the most carefully considered forecasts. Moreover, past practice and experience typically condition organizations of all types to expect linear change or reasonable stability as they look forward. Our human interest in stability, or at least predictability, makes changes in trajectory particularly jolting because they do not conform to our more routine expectations of reality. More often than many of us likely would care to admit, we learn that a market strategy, tactic, or practice no longer works only at the moment it no longer works, leaving us to wonder why.

Still, the limitations of our predictive ability notwithstanding, it is important to consider what the forces of demographic, economic, and cultural change portend for the future of higher education. The broad trends associated with them will assert an inescapable arc of influence for years to come. Changing demography, economics, and cultural values have conspired to fundamentally alter the higher education marketplace, among other things shifting market power from seller (colleges and universities) to buyer (students and families). The days of growth-fueled demand and the broad pricing power it created are over for much of higher education, with the notable exception of elite, big-brand colleges and universities who likely will continue to hold their extraordinary market leadership position as aspirational institutions.

It almost surely is axiomatic in American culture that people of all types and incomes would rather pay less than more while getting more than less. That's true for all types of consumer behavior, including the selection of a college. Students and families increasingly will seek out the highest-value college experiences they can obtain at the best net price point possible. Nothing suggests they will behave otherwise. That, however, ought not to require a race to the economic bottom. The best price point will not always be the lowest price but instead will represent a point of intersection that aligns the financial wherewithal of students and families with their expectations of value and return. Changing marketplace conditions ensure that the price-value nexus will become ever more important. Value truly will be king. And we will have to do a better job than ever before defining and conveying just what value means.

I do not believe that students and families will expect the quality of their college experience to diminish—irrespective of how they define quality. In fact, as the stakes associated with the experience rise, their expectations likely will rise even higher. At the same time, though, we should expect them to press with more urgency and energy to have their collegiate experience delivered at a lower net price. That prevailing sentiment has enormous implications for colleges and universities everywhere. In the coming years, we can expect less enrollment stability, rising price sensitivity, more pricing experimentation, and rising demands for accountability and value—a challenging marketplace to be sure but one for which we must be prepared. Three broad trends in the higher education marketplace surely will require the full attention of college leaders in the coming years.

1. Overall demand for postsecondary education will remain very high, but college enrollment will become increasingly less predictable and stable

The cost of attending college notwithstanding, there is no preparatory alternative to a postsecondary education that offers a greater or even similar opportunity for economic sustainability and success. Recent reports from both the Federal Reserve Bank of New York[1] and the Federal Reserve Bank of Cleveland[2] clearly make the point: the economic benefits of college continue to outweigh its costs. On average, labor markets continue to reward the skills and experiences associated with higher levels of educational attainment with greater job opportunities, more employment security, and higher immediate and lifetime earnings.[3] Students and families fully understand that opportunity—as do secondary schools, whose primary purpose today, for better or for worse, has become the preparation of young people for postsecondary education. No social or labor market trends suggest that the economic returns to increasing education will suddenly reverse or vanish in America. Instead, in the absence of a widely available substitute offering similar economic opportunities, we can expect total demand for higher education to remain very strong. That's the good news.

But it is not all good or easy news. While overall demand for postsecondary education will remain high, the combined effects of changing demography and economic insecurity have reshaped the admission marketplace in ways that perhaps paradoxically weaken the ability of colleges and universities to meet their enrollment goals and limit their ability to understand annual enrollment performance.

Responding to the economic cues of the labor market, young people have flocked to college at historically high rates, and many institutions have experienced tremendous increases in admission application volume over the last decade. But peeling the onion skin back a bit, it is clear that prospective students increasingly hedge their college bets by applying to more institutions. In fall 2012, more than half of all first-time new entering students at four-year colleges and universities in the United States applied for admission to at least five institutions, up from 37 percent in fall 2000 and just 26 percent in fall 1990.[4] While in past years, many colleges and universities could feel secure (or not) about their new entering class by early April, today May 1—the de facto national "signing day" for college admission—has more of the characteristics of a day of reckoning. It is not unusual for colleges to receive half or more of their enrollment deposits in the days immediately before and after May 1, making May Day a source of extraordinarily high anxiety. Will we or won't we make it successfully to the finish line?

What makes May 1 now so frightening is that our ability to understand real demand and predict admission yield has declined, and will continue to decline at many colleges and universities, as students apply to more and more institutions. The proportion of students who apply to five or more colleges has doubled since 1990. The array of choices they consider is remarkable—and sometimes nonsensical to casual and even seasoned observers. I often have wondered when talking to prospective students how they determined where to apply to college, particularly when their lists of submitted applications are populated by institutions that not only seem but often are completely different from each other in size, scope, and mission. I suspect the answer lies not so much with the broadening interests of students but rather with the changing ways and means that colleges and universities approach them in the marketplace. We send out more search mail than ever before designed to entice the interest of more students than ever before, and we have fully utilized the Internet to simplify the application process and reduce barriers to it. Those tactics have worked well; students clearly have responded to our invitation beyond what anyone could have imagined twenty or even ten years ago.

But more may not always be better. As prospective students have added more institutions to their list for consideration, they likely have made it more difficult to settle comfortably on a final choice.[5] The percentage of students nationally who report landing at their first-choice college or university has plummeted as the number of colleges to which they apply has risen. In fall 1990, when only one-quarter of all new four-year college students applied for admission to five or more institutions, 71 percent reported that they enrolled at their top-choice school. Back in those days, fully one-quarter of all new students applied to just one institution, presumably settling on their choice as a condition for application. By 2012, when more than half of all new students applied to at least five institutions, only 59 percent said they enrolled at their first-choice school.[6] At my institutions, the College of Saint Benedict and Saint John's University, our new students who apply to the most institutions (five or more) are more than 20 percentage points less likely than their classmates who apply to four or fewer schools to cite us as their first-choice school (89% vs. 67%). Rather than expanding opportunity, it may well be that more options have led to diminished clarity about the final choice—which in turn has diminished clarity about our yield expectations.

The seeming rise in admission demand—expressed by increasing numbers of applications—has for many institutions been wholly offset by a sharp decline in admission yield. Our experiences in Minnesota are telling and ominous. Between fall 2007 and fall 2012, applications for admission to Minnesota's seventeen private colleges and universities collectively rose by 23 percent, a cause for celebration on campuses throughout the state. The number of applicants accepted for admission at those institutions rose by 15 percent—a sign that they collectively tried to find a comfortable balance between increased selectivity and yield security. Though experiences varied considerably by institution, as a group, Minnesota's private colleges appeared well positioned for extraordinary enrollment success.

The final enrollment numbers tell a more complicated story. In spite of the run-up in applications and acceptances, total enrollment of first-time new entering students at the seventeen colleges was nearly 0.5 percent lower in fall 2012 than it had been in fall 2007. The substantial increase in demand—expressed by rising numbers of applications for admission and generated by significant financial investments in admission marketing and outreach—produced no net gain in enrollment across the association. Since fall 2007, the composite yield rate among students accepted at a private college or university in Minnesota has declined by 5 percentage points. It has fallen by 10 percentage points since 2000.[7] No institution has had a singularly bad experience over the last decade, but all have had to wrestle with a new and much more uncertain marketplace where application numbers are no longer suggestive of a strong result.

Because the root phenomenon—the trend to higher multiple applications for admission—is common everywhere, this story surely could be repeated at private and public colleges and universities across the country. Nothing about the future enrollment marketplace, where the number of domestic high school graduates will flatten out and family economic uncertainty will persist, suggests any improvement. Prospective students will continue to explore a large number of collegiate options in the hopes of finding the one that best balances their personal price-value nexus. As a result, for many institutions the annual challenge of reconciling high demand with declining yield will remain a front-and-center issue for years to come, a task made considerably more difficult in a buyer's market.

2. Families will remain highly price sensitive and demand will rise for more financial assistance

The high and rising price of college has become such an overriding national concern that, even if the rate of price increase slows—and it almost surely will, at least in the short term, in response to intense market pressure—we still should expect rising price sensitivity among students and families. Increased sensitivity to price has been and will continue to be driven by both changing demography and changing economic circumstances. It will unfold in a number of key ways, though its effects will not be uniform for all institutions. For that reason, it behooves college and university leaders to develop a keen understanding of the price elasticity of demand in their particular markets as they devise enrollment strategy.[8] It is a mistake to assume that demand will remain a constant in a changing marketplace.

More families will seek financial assistance and demonstrate financial need. "Need" for purposes of awarding financial aid often is a poorly understood concept outside of the financial aid office. Aid application forms are complex and foreign to many families and the formulas used to determine ability to pay seem, and in many ways are, both mysterious and arcane. My own conversations with families suggest that most fill out their college financial aid applications with equal measures of fear and faith and little sense of understanding about what the completed process might actually yield. They cross their fingers and hope for the best—an approach often shared by many campus leaders, as well.

At its simplest, financial need reflects the difference between adjudicated ability to pay (which is derived from information about family income, family assets, family size, and the number of children in college) and the posted total price of attendance, including tuition, fees, room, board, and other college-going costs. In theory, though not always in practice, ability to pay remains the same irrespective of the institution a student chooses to attend. If I have a derived ability to pay of $10,000 at the University of X, then I should have the same or similar ability to pay at the College of Y, independent of the price of either. My financial need varies among the various institutions to which I apply for admission only because the price of attendance varies.

In theory these concepts are all rather neat. In reality they more often are sources of extraordinary anxiety, particularly as the price of college has risen faster than family income. Financial aid professionals at all types of institutions can tell tales of families who believe they need at least some assistance to pay for college, irrespective of the ability-to-pay numbers that tumble out of the financial aid application process. It is easy to understand why for lower-income and most middle-income families. The pre–financial aid price of sending even one child to college often represents an enormous share of their family income, whether they choose a public or private college or university.

The price of college is an equal opportunity fear. Financial concerns persist even for families who by most economic standards would be considered well-off. At my institutions last fall, fully two-thirds of parents of first-year students whose family income exceeded $100,000 indicated that the cost of college after financial aid was a very important consideration in their college decision. More than 1 in 4 said they would have enrolled elsewhere for less than $5,000 in additional grant or scholarship assistance from their second choice, a perilously thin margin in a competitive marketplace. A similar percentage of these same families indicated that they had a *major* concern about their ability to finance their daughter or son's college education through to completion.

Like federal and state income tax rates, expected ability to pay for college goes up as income and wealth increase. No magic there. The formulas are quite progressive; if you have more resources, you will be expected to pay more for college (all other things remaining equal, of course). Financial aid formulas are very good at identifying families with little ability to pay for college, the families who should and most often do receive the greatest assistance. However, because the expectations built into the formulas rise quickly for families with incomes over $75,000, they create an efficacy concern among families who would otherwise describe themselves as middle-class or even upper-middle-class. They very often approach us with the very simple question, "Can this be real?"

A simple example illustrates the point. Federal financial aid formulas—which use data provided by families on the Free Application for Federal Student Aid (FAFSA)—judge that a family of four with one child in college and an adjusted gross income of approximately $140,000 should be able to pay the full price of attendance at an institution priced at or around $45,000 (inclusive of tuition, fees, room, board, and other college-related expenses).[9] By formula, that family would not demonstrate need at an institution priced at that point. In reality, the family almost surely won't believe that conclusion. Most parents will instead reasonably and passionately argue that they do not have the equivalent of one-third of their pretax family income available to send their daughter or son to college, a concern made more pressing when considered in relation to children who may be next in line for college.

Formulas and algorithms are, of course, deeply impersonal. But real-life families are not, and even those with higher levels of income often do not believe they have the resources available to finance the total cost of college for their children without at least some assistance. Clearly institutions cannot and should not wantonly hand out grants and scholarships to families from whom it is reasonable to expect a significant financial effort. That is, after all, why financial aid formulas were developed years ago. At the same time, though, we cannot assume that price sensitivity is limited only to those in the bottom half of the income distribution. Nor should we assume that financial aid formulas produce an expected ability-to-pay result that yields a realistic or believable outcome at all levels of family income and wealth. Intra-industry debates about the efficacy of need-based grants versus non-need-based scholarships—debates that often are quite intense—represent little more than inside baseball to families who seek assistance in some form, any form, to help pay for college for their children.

All colleges and universities ultimately are subject to the following equation: when the price of college rises faster than family income or ability to pay, someone who had been able to pay without assistance before the increase now requires assistance and someone who had not been able to pay prior to the increase requires even greater assistance than before. The math and logic are quite simple and straightforward. And, unfortunately, often very costly both to families and to institutions. The number of students receiving financial assistance is rising, as are the amounts they are awarded. Research by the US Department of Education indicates that in 2009–10, 82 percent of students attending public four-year colleges and universities and 89 percent of students attending private four-year not-for-profit institutions received some form of financial assistance (with student loans comprising between one-third and half of the total aid received).[10] Both percentages were higher than they had been in 2006–07—a useful prerecession, post-recession comparison. The amount of financial aid awarded has risen much faster than the number receiving aid, a reflection of the changing marketplace. Data collected by the College Board in 2012 indicated that total federal, state, institutional, and private financial aid awarded to undergraduate students in the United States rose by 58 percent between 2007–08 (the beginning of the recession) and 2011–12.[11] The largest increases were in federal grant aid awarded to undergraduates, which more than doubled; federal student borrowing, which increased by 49 percent; and, increases in institutionally awarded grants and scholarships, which increased by 38 percent.

If the price of college continues to rise faster than family income or the value of family assets, and it likely will if only because incomes in particular are not rising or rising only slowly, most colleges and universities can expect a growing number of families seeking financial aid and demonstrating financial need, which will require additional financial aid. More significantly, the changing socioeconomic characteristics of the rising generation of traditional-age college students—who are more racially and ethnically diverse than ever before but much more likely to come from families with lower incomes—ensures that demands for significant financial assistance will continue to escalate, even if colleges and universities are able to reduce the rate of their price increases. The conclusion is clear. Barring remarkable and sustained changes in pricing practice, large-scale investments in financial aid are here to stay.

Net price, value sensitivity, and the art of the deal will become increasingly central to college choice among all types of students and families. Price sensitivity is already high among new students and their families. In fall 2012, two-thirds of all new entering students at four-year colleges in the United States agreed that the "current economic situation" had significantly influenced their college choice.[12] Institutional deselection based on price—real or perceived—is already widespread and rising. More than half (52%) of all traditional-age undergraduate students in 2012 indicated that they had eliminated a college before applying because of cost, up sharply from 42 percent in 2008.[13] Nearly 4 in 10 said they had eliminated a school from consideration after submitting their admission application (up from 27% in 2008), and half ruled out an institution based on its net price after having received a financial aid package (up from 38% in 2008). In other words, most undergraduate students today eliminate prospective institutions at some point based on price alone.

Demographic and economic trends suggest that even fewer students in the years ahead will have the financial resources required to pay for college unaided. Together with the significant ongoing concern about the rising price of college, we can expect increasing price sensitivity at the point of choice as students and families seek to stretch their budgets to meet college costs and maximize value. These trends present particularly significant challenges to institutions that are tuition dependent and lack a strong brand-driven market position or other highly differentiating market characteristic. Rising price sensitivity not only threatens enrollment—I may lose more students to institutions at a lower net price point—it also will put increasing downward pressure on net tuition revenue, already a significant challenge at private and public colleges and universities across the country.

That families who already demonstrate need will require even more financial assistance as the price of college rises should not come as a surprise to anyone. However, it is a serious mistake to assume that families with the greatest means will willingly continue to pay the full and rising price of college anywhere without some financial inducement or support. Their perceptions of value may lag their resources. Retail giants like Target, Wal-Mart, and Costco have built tremendously successful—and now ubiquitous—business enterprises on the singular assumption of pay less, get more. High ability to pay does not always translate into high willingness to pay, and college and university leaders must be increasingly attentive to the value expectations (or, in economic terms, the price elasticity of demand) of their higher-income students. To make the equation even more difficult, expectations of value at the undergraduate level today may also be considered in the context of graduate school expectations: If I wish to pursue a graduate degree, can I afford to make this undergraduate choice?

Pricing power results from both demand volume and perceptions of value. The gravest sin for an institution is to assume it has pricing power when in fact it does not. As price rises, it is reasonable to anticipate that expectations of value also will rise. When a posted price is higher than expectations of value for any good or service, consumers of all incomes will either expect a discounted price or they will shop elsewhere. That is as true in higher education, where choices are plentiful, as it is in retail enterprise. Colleges and universities can expect to see more high-means families in their financial aid offices making a case for assistance or inducements as the price of college escalates and perceptions of value change or struggle to keep up. We will have to be prepared with a response that recognizes our market position and balances our enrollment goals with our need for net revenue and our institutional values.

More colleges and universities will experiment with price. Price setting typically is a time-consuming, often angst-ridden, exercise at colleges and universities, becoming more so in recent years as economic pressures have mounted. Yet in spite of the lengthy conversations and mathematical modeling that drive and define the process, it very often yields a consistent and similar outcome across the marketplace. Similar types of institutions, particularly those competing in the same markets for the same students, typically raise their prices at similar rates and go to market with similar comprehensive prices. The prices and price changes do not reflect shared planning or, worse, collusion, but instead result from common cost structures and pressures and a common understanding of the market. Over a long period of time, most institutions have learned what types of students and families have been able and willing to consider their educational experience. In other words, price setting very often reflects a behavior borne of market understanding and familiarity: particular kinds of students and families will seek particular kinds of colleges and universities within a particular range of prices. That market experience often is shared among many institutions.

Public and private institutions set price differently, though the purpose of price setting is similar at both. In addition to considerations of markets and cost structures, price at public colleges and universities also is shaped by levels of taxpayer support and the level of price control exercised by public policy makers, both of which vary considerably by state and even by institutional systems within states. Sharp declines in state appropriations for higher education in recent years have very often resulted in steep tuition rate increases at public colleges and universities as those institutions have sought to recoup at least a portion of their lost revenue. However, few public institutions have the autonomous flexibility to raise their price as they see fit in response to changes in state appropriations without legislative approval or input. Legislative pressure—often under the auspices of consumer protection—acts as a constraint on the ability of leaders at public colleges and universities to raise their price of attendance (at least for in-state students). Private colleges and universities, on the other hand, generally do not receive direct operating subsidies from taxpayers and are not subject to legislative oversight on price. They must engage the marketplace directly when they set price—also a risky proposition given that their starting price position most often is higher than it is at public institutions. In either case, though, the mediating influence of taxpayer support or legislative governance notwithstanding, both public and private institutions ultimately seek to set a price point designed to succeed in the markets in which they compete and to generate the resources they need to effectively serve the students they enroll.

But what happens when markets change and pricing practices no longer yield the same positive effects? Changing demographic and economic conditions are sure to lead to more price experimentation in the coming years, particularly for institutions who find themselves most at risk in the new marketplace or increasingly subject to public policy constraints. Are we priced appropriately to the students we seek to enroll? Will we have the ability to replace taxpayer resources with tuition? Can we continue to raise our price at this rate? How much pricing capacity do we have with the students we seek to enroll? Does our price point provide us with an opportunity to generate the resources we need to operate as we expect? Are we overpriced or underpriced with all or at least some of our students? Can we afford to behave like everybody else in the marketplace? How does our pricing strategy position us for the future? If state resources are declining but our authority to raise price is limited, what changes must we consider? College and university leaders often ask questions like these—and should ask them—but they will be posed with increasing frequency and urgency over the next decade.

Looking forward, we can expect that more colleges and universities will engage in price-bending exercises to meet the needs, demands, and imperatives of their markets and their publics. Price experimentation likely will be popular—a kind of first-line antibiotic—because price is more easily manipulated than spending and often has an immediate effect in the marketplace and on student choice behavior. Strategies like tuition reductions,[14] tuition freezes, more highly differentiated pricing by program or activity (including things like housing and amenities), and even greater increases in student financial aid all will receive more attention. None of these strategies is new, but we can expect to see them more often and expressed in more varied ways as a larger number of institutions seek to adapt to the new marketplace. Each strategy carries considerable risk, though for most colleges maintaining the status quo has its own risks. Institutions who by choice or by market force implement new pricing strategies must carefully and realistically lay out the risks and rewards of those choices, reconciling both their short-term and long-term strategic expectations as well as their revenue and expense needs.

3. Students, families, and the public at large will express rising outcome expectations and demand accountability in increasingly strong terms

Expectations of higher education already are very high. Students and families today express them in any number of ways: provide me with a high-quality academic experience; ensure that all of the courses I want and need are available, preferably at a time of my choosing; make sure I have access to the latest and greatest technology; provide me with extensive academic and personal counseling services; house me comfortably and provide me with lots of options but ensure that I get my first choice; provide me with many amenities, like great food, great recreational facilities, and great entertainment opportunities; prepare me for and help me to obtain a good paying job after college as well as for career advancement. And so on.

These are not completely unreasonable demands. Though they are sometimes described as the narcissistic impulses of the current marketplace, colleges and universities everywhere have individually and collectively helped to create and feed them, not only to satisfy market expectations but also to build sources of competitive advantage for our individual institutions. But taken altogether they often test both our purposes and, increasingly, our budgets. Like the old Army recruitment slogan, we very often are expected to "be all you can be." For all people and to all people. More important for planning purposes, these expectations and demands show no signs of abating, and the rising price of college certainly will keep them alive and growing. Unchecked, they will create a circumstance something like the ravenous, murderous plant, Audrey, in the play *Little Shop of Horrors,* who must continually be fed, ultimately to everyone's detriment. Few institutions will be able to indefinitely sustain the costs of infinitely rising expectations of the collegiate experience. The central questions for the next decade will be what are the alternatives and how do we manage them?

My colleague Cal Mosley is an extraordinary observer of markets. He has for more than forty years played a leadership role at both highly selective and less selective institutions developing recruitment strategy and engaging families in the college recruitment process. Over those many years, he has learned, sometimes the hard way, that markets (writ large) most often are unsentimental and uninterested in particular institutional issues or problems, especially the issues that attract so much attention at executive leadership gatherings and board meetings. As they progress through their college search process, students and families by and large express little interest in or concern about the challenges colleges may face in meeting salary benchmarks, or balancing competing budget priorities, or that an institution may be underendowed, or that the tuition discount rate may be rising at an unsustainable pace, or that state government resources may have been slashed. Those are issues for institutional leadership to resolve, and if a college cannot deliver a quality experience at a manageable price point in relation to rising expectations of value, then so be it. Students and families will move on to the next choice. There are other institutions from which to choose.

All colleges want (and very often need) prospective students to fall in love with their institutions. The language and tactics of admission efforts are designed to produce that emotion. However, from the vantage point of the economic marketplace, romanticism will almost always take a back seat to more hard-hearted reality. At the end of the day, you either meet my needs and expectations or you don't. Students and families ultimately vote with their feet (and their wallets) to send signals about their perceptions and experiences of value. That's the way markets work. Those signals can be immediate or play out over a long period of time, but in either case, institutional leaders must be attentive to them.

But expectations about performance and value are not expressed exclusively through the market choices of students and families. Public policy makers at both the federal and state levels also play an increasingly significant role, weighing in on the value and performance of higher education, often expressing their interest through regulatory action.

It should now be clear to all higher education leaders that the federal and state regulatory train has left the station and isn't coming back. As the stakes associated with a college education have risen, so too has the demand for regulation of higher education. The days of independence and self-direction are long over and all colleges and universities, public and private, will have to continuously adapt to rising public policy expectations and demands.

The Higher Education Act, originally enacted in 1965 and regularly reauthorized since then, governs most federal action in higher education. Most importantly, it shapes the rules and limits of federal investment in higher education, among other things defining eligibility for access to federal financial aid resources. Money is always a powerful lever.

Regulatory oversight has increased continuously since the 1988 reauthorization of the Higher Education Act, when the financial aid needs analysis (and therefore the common standard for deriving ability to pay) was largely federalized. Though it began with more active involvement in financial aid policy, Congress since then has rarely turned away from opportunities to assert a larger government role in the oversight and management of higher education. Most state legislatures have followed suit. The regulation often has been constructed in response to claims of mismanagement or mistrust. And so, higher education in America today finds itself in a position similar to what the health care industry has experienced for the better part of the last two decades: what it provides is nearly universally lionized as a necessity and a gateway experience to economic sustainability, but what it does and how it does it increasingly are demonized as inefficient, ineffective, or even corrupt.

Education leaders everywhere face an increasingly hard-set public perception that college is necessary but not a very good value. It does not help that college leaders often do not express their own case for value particularly well. A 2011 survey conducted by the Pew Research Center of more than 1,000 public and private four-year and two-year college presidents indicated that fewer than one-quarter of all institutional leaders said that the value students get for the money they spend on a college education today is greater than it was ten years ago. More than 4 in 10 rated the value as similar to what it was a decade ago, and fully one-third described it as less valuable.[15] Not a very hopeful message from the executive leadership of American higher education after a period of rapidly rising price, particularly in a marketplace already predisposed to skepticism about cost and value.

Disconnection between perceptions of value and the price of the experience create ripe conditions for a political call to arms. When people feel trapped ("I must have this experience, but the price barriers to access are too high"), they often seek outlets for support, action, and change. And the end result often is political and regulatory intervention.

The higher education associations in Washington, DC, and in state capitals around the country work hard on their members' behalf to address and manage the rising tide of regulation. It's a tough game to play. The issue is no longer how to avoid regulatory intervention but rather how to shape it and live with it as best we can. The 2008 Higher Education Opportunity Act included a smorgasbord of regulatory change, some of it new, some of it refinement of existing law, but collectively a massive assertion of federal oversight. Among other things, the 2008 legislation addressed voter registration, transfer of credit policy, textbook information, net price calculations, fire safety notification, lobbying certification, missing student notification, teacher preparation, cost transparency, copyright infringement, gainful employment, emergency response planning, and financial aid simplification. Congress allocates billions of dollars each year in support of higher education. State governments allocate billions more. The *quid pro quo* clearly is rising.

Much of the regulation has been promulgated not in the name of improved educational quality but rather under the broad umbrella of consumer protection. The primary focus of regulatory action thus far has been oversight of the behavior of colleges and universities rather than specification of particular college outcomes (though that often is cited as a secondary outcome of regulatory intervention). The distinction is important and significant. Leadership and administrative management, not the learning experience, most often have been the targets of regulatory intervention.

Regulatory requirements are remarkably democratic. On most issues, they treat all colleges and universities in the same way; the greatest and the least are subject to similar expectations. For better or for worse, increased regulation may be the price of success. Industries producing something that is or is perceived to be a necessity (particularly a high-stakes necessity) often are subject to high levels of government oversight and regulation, like utilities, health care, and banking, to name just a few. Social or economic necessity typically invites greater scrutiny. And if that weren't enough, large-scale public investments—in higher education's case, billions of taxpayer dollars—ensure the active engagement and fiduciary oversight of public policy makers.

Colleges and universities should not expect the regulatory zeal at either the federal or state levels to diminish anytime soon. We need look no further than federal and state legislation governing elementary and secondary education as an example of what could be. Three things seem clear as we move forward:

1. As the demand for access to higher education increases and the expectations of colleges and universities rise, public policy makers will continue to intervene to manage the relationship between students, families, employers, and colleges. Colleges will not be the beneficiaries of most of that intervention. Instead, they often will play the role of political foil or football.

2. No college will escape the reach of rising federal and state oversight and intervention. It is the price to pay for requesting and accepting significant taxpayer support for students and institutional enterprises. Colleges and universities will have to adapt to those expectations,

which will require more, not fewer, human resources to ensure compliance with the increasing flow of rules and regulations (which has the ironic effect of also increasing expense, and therefore cost, pressure).

3. The cost of college remains the chief concern of most policy makers because it is central to most families. Institutions should expect politicians to pay close attention to the concerns of their voting constituents. Moreover, policy makers fully understand the broad macroeconomic stakes associated with postsecondary educational access and completion. The value of a highly educated and productive populace is rarely a source of dispute. Though up to now they mostly have expressed frustration and anger with rising college prices and have not taken direct action to control them, barring independent changes in price or pricing practice, which are complex and not particularly transparent, policy makers will continue to devote creative energy to managing the rising price of college.

Higher education, of course, is not a blameless victim of regulatory intervention. Our seeming inability to clearly or convincingly bridge the cost-value nexus, in particular, has contributed much to the subsequent action directed at us. However, rather than simply grumbling about the pain and cost of regulatory oversight, we should keep in mind that it is our responsibility to provide the college experience and our opportunity to convey its value in compelling and convincing ways. We will need to seize that opportunity as an imperative to get ahead of the regulatory train rather than to simply fall under it.

CHAPTER SEVEN

Toward a New Marketplace

It is possible to build a great institution that sustains exceptional performance for multiple decades, perhaps longer, even in the face of chaos, disruption, uncertainty and violent change. We are not imprisoned by our circumstances, our setbacks, our history, our mistakes, or even staggering defeats along the way. We are freed by our choices.

—Jim Collins, *How the Mighty Fall*

How are we to lead and behave in a new and complicated environment?

New students with new needs and demands, scarce family and institutional resources, heightened competition, rising expectations for better performance and management. No college or university will have the luxury of wholly avoiding the demographic, economic, and cultural forces reshaping the marketplace today. And yet, there is a something-old-something-new quality to it all. This is not the first disruptive period for higher education nor will it be the last. We have faced these kinds of challenges—sometimes expressed in similar ways, sometimes not—many times before over the last century. Our history as institutions and as an industry has been characterized by an ability to innovate, adapt, and subsequently thrive in response to change. But that can happen only after we wrap our minds around the demands of a new operating environment and then acted assertively in response.

The forces of disruption are both every institution's story and no institution's story. On the one hand, they present inescapable choices and challenges for colleges and universities across the country. They are too deep, too broad, and too powerful to ignore or wish away. On the other hand, they will impact different institutions in vastly different ways. No two institutions will or should approach them from the same vantage point or the have the same set of choices. Which is why, in spite of the swirl of uncertainty that characterizes the new marketplace, two things remain crystal clear. First, colleges and university leaders must have a deep and realistic understanding of their own markets, history, and culture, as well as their own unique opportunities and constraints. Second, solutions suggesting easy answers or that one approach will work for all institutions, tempting as they may seem, are snake oil. All choices and responses must be tuned to a particular context. And most of those choices will present difficult trade-offs.

The changing market conditions demand our full institutional attention and require a considered response. We must address the realities of our particular environment in forward-thinking, grounded, and assertive ways. That is fundamentally a leadership exercise. The endgame is quite clear: aspirational ambitions must be aligned, likely realigned, with financial realities. The moment a college is no longer willing or able to adjust its curricular, cocurricular, or administrative operations to meet its aspirations, it must change its aspirations. Reality will always prevail. In spite of punditry portending ruin, the question for most colleges and universities will not be whether they survive but rather how well they will adapt to succeed in a new and infinitely more complex marketplace.

Disruptive Adaptation

Most colleges and universities will spend the better part of the next decade, not just the next year or two, addressing these issues. The ways we choose to respond to the demands and imperatives of the new marketplace will make all the difference in the world, both to our future students and to our institutions. While innovation likely will play a role in future planning and success, adaptation will play an even larger role: given who we are and how we operate, how will we adapt our mission, market, and management practice to the realities of a new marketplace and a world of new and perhaps different expectations? The issue is not merely about survival but rather about how to best position our institution to ensure that it provides students with exceptional learning and developmental opportunities that prepare them to achieve their goals and dreams.

The deep and cross-cutting pressures of disruption will require some amount of adaptation at every college and university in the United States. That process can be framed along three basic lines:

1. *Market adaptation,* identifying new markets for students, new ways to succeed in current markets, and new or alternative pricing practices. Each of these options presents an array of complex choices. New markets typically take years to develop, particularly those at a great distance or those requiring enrollment of students who have never before considered the institution as a real option. New ways to succeed in current markets requires a competitive leap forward. You must best your competition in a meaningful way, most often at the same time they are trying to best you. New pricing practices require a sophisticated financial calculus and a deep understanding of the relationship of demand, value, and budget practice. Any form of market adaptation requires the simultaneous consideration and alignment of market goals, market strength, and mission imperatives.

2. *Management adaptation,* involving a combination of new pathways to efficiency and productivity and new ways of delivering and supporting the infrastructure of the institution. The subject of innumerable business texts, management adaptation requires not only a careful assessment of the opportunities and limitations of productivity improvement but also a commitment to understanding how the various offices, departments, and activities of a college or university—inclusive of mission-central and support activities—contribute to the comprehensive purposes of the institution. We too often view our management choices as discrete or serial choices, rather than examining them in the broader context of their integrated contribution to our overall purpose and effectiveness. We also too often think of management and program choices through an accretive prism, which makes efforts to rescale or refocus particularly challenging.

3. *Learning adaptation,* exploring new ways of imagining and delivering the educational experience, including new approaches to pedagogy, new curricula, new or different degree requirements, and new or different educational partnerships. Learning adaptation likely offers the most fertile ground for change, since it links central mission commitments to both market opportunity and management practice. However, it also presents the set of choices most burdened with the

weight and trajectory of institutional history and values. More so than market or management adaptation, learning adaptation often demands changes in highly valued educational practices or a willingness to give up some control of the curriculum, neither of which comes easily to traditional colleges and universities. Curricular content and learning delivery is highly decentralized at most institutions and the nearly exclusive province of the faculty. Command and control management typical in other industries is not a characteristic of higher education. Faculty engagement and participation must be central to any change in the learning experience. Faculty, administrative leaders, and trustees must work together to effect any meaningful change in the learning experience. Intellectual autonomy is not limited only to faculty and academic departments, however. Institutions as a whole also operate with a great deal of independence. They have a proprietary interest in their own learning experience, their own programs and activities, and their own facilities, all of which can make partnerships difficult to negotiate and navigate. Learning adaptation can only occur within the cultural confines of a particular institution.

None of the three vectors of adaptation are independent; choices in one influence choices in the others. Institutional conditions will, and should, determine the particular type and degree of change required. Most importantly, market adaptation, management adaptation, and learning adaptation should not occur in a vacuum. The purposes and objectives of any adaptive change must be clearly specified, and consideration must be given to any interactive effects or downstream consequences they create. A few key questions are required for strategic decision making:

— Does this action achieve the objectives we have identified? How will we know it has achieved those purposes?
— Does it create harmful externalities or unintended consequences? If it does, how can we mitigate those effects?
— Is the choice sustainable over a desired period of time?
— Do the benefits associated with the action exceed the difficulty required to enact it?

These are not uncommon questions unique to higher education. They would appear in any strategic planning guide. Still, it is important to keep them front and center to ensure they do not devolve to rhetorical expressions quickly brushed aside. The questions should be asked and answered prior to the point of decision making—particularly for high-stakes choices. Illustrations of poor or failed choices are easy to imagine; every institution can identify its own list. The key to managing the risk associated with making choices is to create processes and practices that require integrated thinking, decision making, and management.

The Anatomy of Decision

How institutions frame decisions is as important as the choices they ultimately make. Decision-making frameworks and *a priori* assumptions can aid creative thinking but just as often constrain it. Intellectual inertia, risk aversion, and an inability to think in an integrated way collectively comprise significant threats to good decision making in organizations everywhere. Each has the effect of limiting choice, often in damaging ways, by reducing thinking to preconceived boxes drawn mostly from the temple of the familiar. We've never done it that way. We can't do it that way. We have always done it alone. Each forms an all too common recipe for poor decision making.

The graphic below lays out a series of mission, market, and management choices—clustered in ways that represent common choice sets at colleges and universities—in terms of the degree of difficulty associated with a choice and the impact that might result from making it.[1] The map is neither a complete nor an objective depiction of the variety of choices a college or university could make. The impact and difficulty of any of these choices (or any other set of choices) clearly will depend on the conditions and characteristics particular to the institution. Still, it provides a useful visual rubric for framing and comparing the budget and program choice options most colleges and universities actually make.

The terms of the map are important. The difficulty axis demands an understanding of the effort required to make the change. What will it take financially to make this choice? What types of organizational processes are required to make it happen? Who are the stakeholders and who needs to be involved in the decision-making process? How much political capital must I expend and with whom to reach a successful conclusion? These questions are critical to all types of decisions but particularly to high-stakes decisions that cut across managerial or divisional lines within an institution.

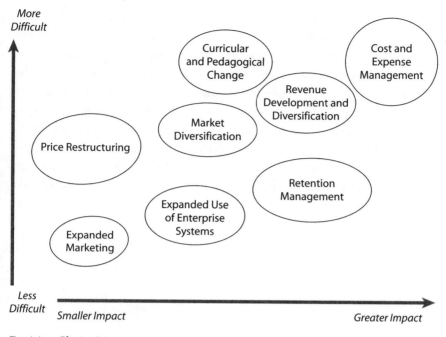

More
Difficult

Curricular
and Pedagogical
Change

Cost and
Expense
Management

Revenue
Development and
Diversification

Market
Diversification

Price Restructuring

Retention
Management

Expanded Use
of Enterprise
Systems

Expanded
Marketing

Less
Difficult

Smaller Impact

Greater Impact

Decision Choice Map

The impact axis requires an understanding not only of the financial, brand, market, human resource, or program outcomes expected but also the externalities, positive or negative, created by the choice. All choices carry with them consequences that extend beyond the narrow confines of a particular action. For example, if I plan to increase my enrollment by seeking more international students, the impact goes well beyond the financial or human capital investments in admission strategy to achieve that goal. I also must consider the implications and costs for residence life or academic advising or student support services that likely will result from achieving it. Similarly, while a particular program reduction may result in significant budget savings, I must also consider its impact on admission strategy, or perhaps even development strategy. In either case, decision making must be conditioned to take into account both the immediate and peripheral effects of a particular choice.

The axes of the chart attempt to integrate expected effort with expected outcomes. Their relationship must be at least proportional, with the easiest choices those that require little effort but yield a significant positive impact—the kind of action typically described as "low-hanging fruit." However, most choices are not so clear or easy. The map provides an opportunity for simultaneous consideration of any number of seemingly unrelated choices—the kinds of choices that college and university leaders need to make in real life and real time. The level of effort or amount of impact associated with a particular choice matters less than the net effect of effort and impact considered together. The value of the expected outcome must exceed the cost of obtaining it, cost that can and should be evaluated in terms of financial capital, human capital, physical capital, and political capital. No choice or decision comes without a price, and price and reward must always be considered in tandem.

CHAPTER EIGHT

Reimagine the Future

Think. Different.

Here's to the crazy ones. The misfits. The rebels. The troublemakers. The round pegs in the square holes. The ones who see things differently. They're not fond of rules. And they have no respect for the status quo. You can quote them, disagree with them, glorify or vilify them. About the only thing you can't do is ignore them. Because they change things. They push the human race forward. And while some may see them as the crazy ones, we see genius. Because the people who are crazy enough to think they can change the world are the ones who do.

—Apple, "Think Different"

The surest way of ruining a youth is to teach him to respect those who think as he does more highly than those who think differently.

—Friedrich Nietzsche, *Daybreak*

For more than forty years, the academic calendar at the College of Saint Benedict and Saint John's University operated on a six-day class cycle delivered in a week that ran from Monday to Monday but did not include weekends. Classes were identified as occurring on 1-3-5 days or 2-4-6 days. As the cycle played out over the semester, any day of the week could be one of those numbers. The regular academic day offered five class periods, each seventy minutes long. Labs generally occurred in the afternoons and could be scheduled on any day of the week. From the vantage point of a student, it wasn't particularly complicated to remember once having gotten used to it. Since most students enrolled in four courses per semester, generally taking two classes per day, each class would typically occur three times per week one week, followed by two the next week, and so on.

By 2012, few people on campus remained who could describe exactly why that particular, and peculiar, class schedule had been created or whether the benefits initially considered remained benefits at all. But after four decades, it was clear that the class cycle had become more than an organizing principle. It was part of the colleges' self-identity. Not everyone liked it, but everyone knew it and had become accustomed to it. It was unique—or at least not shared by any of the colleges' competitors, peers, or aspirants. Over time, it had evolved from a "what is" to something more like a "what must be." Until, in 2012, new Academic Dean Richard Ice asked, "Why do we build our schedule this way?"

No single event led him to that question, which had been asked a number of times in prior years. However, Dean Ice saw the writing on the wall as student needs and interests had changed. More and more students sought internships and off-campus experiences. Those opportunities and experiences operated on a standard working calendar, where Monday meant Monday, not a number 1 through 6 that varied by day and by week. The unusual class schedule limited opportunities for many students because they could not construct a routine employment schedule for their internships or a regular working schedule for service learning. As more students expected internships and off-campus experiences, and as the colleges sought to expand those opportunities, the class cycle had become an impediment. In a move of unusual speed, and with unusual consensus, Dean Ice fast-tracked the issue and championed it through the academic decision-making process. A little more than a year later, the class cycle and academic calendar were changed, transforming the rhythm of life on campus and expanding learning opportunities off campus. It took one determined, respected, and well-placed person to ask "why" and "what if" to change something that had been considered up to that point essentially unalterable.

Genomics, Part I

Organizations of all types, including colleges and universities, approach decision making—strategic or tactical, complex or simple—through the lens of a worldview and processes that guide their thinking, shape and reflect their values, and define their sense of self. The prism and practice together provide an anchor point from which we can address all kinds of different issues. Biology provides a useful mnemonic in this case: the stock of values, mores, practices, and traditions that define who our institutions are and how we act might collectively be described as a kind of genome.

The organizational DNA that comprises the higher education genome has developed over hundreds of years as values and practices like shared governance, disciplinary learning, time to degree, pedagogical methods, tenure, the academic calendar, and residential life, among many others, have evolved.[1] Those practices and values were given birth sometimes in the face of changing social conditions, like war or economic calamity, sometimes in the face of changing social values, and other times because of the vision and values of particularly strong and influential leaders (think James Bryant Conant or Clark Kerr). Each step of the way built on, and in some cases substantially altered, what preceded it. Over a long period of time, the evolutionary development of the higher education organizational DNA has been shared widely among institutions of all types. The anchoring power of the institutional genome has sustained colleges and universities for generations. It often protects us from mission drift, capriciousness, and the temptation to continuously lurch in response to the impulses and whims of the moment. As importantly, it provides a crucible for our values. Christensen and Eyring shrewdly note that in higher education the kind of entrepreneurialism often attributed to business leadership is rare but that "this steadiness is a major source of universities' value to a fickle, fad-prone society."[2]

Many of the values and practices that comprise the higher education genome today have taken on an aura similar to natural law, seemingly ordained and just as often seemingly immutable or unalterable. They are baked into the identity of most traditional colleges and universities, guiding our choices and shaping our sense of self-efficacy. We are designed and genetically programmed to be just what we are, to make choices in a particular way, and to behave in particular ways. That is not to say that evolution ever stops, that traditional values and practices always preclude innovation or change, or that all colleges and universities completely share their genome and behave in exactly the same way or share exactly the same values. None of that is true. Still, in the face of disruptive or liminal moments of change, it is particularly important for college and university leaders to consider and acknowledge the anchoring power of their genome and the ways it might constrain their ability to think beyond the temple of the familiar. Failure to think beyond our genome can expose us to a number of important decision-making and leadership traps that can limit our ability to act with dispatch or conviction when changing conditions demand it. A handful of sentiments common to organizations of all types indicate how that can happen.

1. *The world understands and values us the way we understand and value ourselves.* It clearly is important that we believe passionately in what our institutions do and seek to do. We typically explain our purposes and practices in high-minded and even noble language. But it is a mistake to assume that prospective students, parents, college trustees, policy makers, or the world at large see it the same way or appreciate those same values. They very often do not. "They just don't understand" is neither a complete nor an appropriate leadership response—though one I have heard many times over the years in a variety of different settings. The burden of proof rests with institutions to continuously convey the value of what they do and why and how they do it. In the end, the market owns the ultimate trump card: it can and will vote with its feet.

2. *Past is prologue for the future.* History and tradition are important parts of the collegiate experience and our sense of institutional self. A visit to any campus at commencement or convocation, or even football Saturday, clearly expresses that point. We relish our history, sometimes embellish it, and most often seek to preserve it and cast it forward. But in changing times and under difficult circumstances, we must consider the degree to which past practice, tradition, or even folklore act as decision-making constraints. Sentiments like "we don't do things that way" or "we can't consider that or do that" represent the penultimate shutdown response to change, even when change becomes an imperative and inaction a grave threat. They are the bane of every kind of organization.

3. *The primary pathway to better must be through more.* That an institution can generate better results or achieve greater things with more resources is widely accepted as something close to a self-evident truth. However, as a guiding principle it can become a dangerous game that few can win or keep pace. Like an economic production function, as the revenue and spending cycle plays out, more and more resources are required to generate diminishing incremental results. Put more simply, the fire must continuously be stoked with increasingly more fuel and effort just to be maintained. On the other hand, colleges and universities often resist the difficulty, and even pain, typically associated with

contraction. We experience it through the lens of loss, particularly when it involves people, which it inevitably does in higher education. Moreover, contraction in higher education very often is perceived as a sign of market or management weakness or failure. It rarely symbolizes success, either on campus or off campus, even when it may be the best or only choice. Though typically framed, incorrectly, as doing less with less (an almost completely unappealing market proposition) or more with less (an unattainable hope in many cases), in the face of change, contraction is better approached as requiring that we do *differently* with less—which puts the highest premium on gaining the greatest effect possible from any given level of resources. It requires leaders to balance reality and aspiration. In a marketplace demanding change to the basic financial model of higher education, discovering how to do differently (and well) with less will become a leadership imperative.

All college and university leaders could describe how they have experienced each of these arguments at least to some degree at one time or another. Commonly expressed, sometimes explicitly and other times implicitly, each draws its power from firmly embedded organizational DNA. Unfortunately, when they become the prevailing sentiment, they can individually or collectively create a leadership prison that hinders our capacity to make strategic decisions in a competitive, changing, and high-stakes environment. In short, exercised to their ends, they can threaten both the quality and sustainability of our enterprises.

It is not easy to think beyond our genome. It can be difficult even to recognize its anchoring influence because it manifests itself so naturally in long-held, even assumed, values and practices. Still, the ability to look beyond and to understand both the advantages and limitations of our institutional genome is a leadership requirement and a management imperative in the new marketplace for higher education.

Apple

In her insightful book, *Different,* the Harvard Business School's Youngme Moon describes the perils of sameness and the imperative for meaningful differentiation, particularly in crowded markets which feature products or services that are difficult for all but the most discerning or knowledgeable consumers to distinguish. She bemoans the herd-like "me too" mentality that drives and shapes so many industries today: "As the number of products within a category multiplies, the differences between them start to become increasingly trivial, almost to the point of preposterousness. The category has reached the point where it is possible for product heterogeneity to be experienced as product homogeneity. Which is not to say that the distinctions between products are not real; it is simply to say that they are real only in the same way synonyms have discrete connotations . . . [T]his is when it can require a category expert—a connoisseur—to negotiate the category with any kind of ease."[3]

Moon's vivid summary ought to make us uncomfortable in higher education because, while she does not single out colleges and universities as perpetrators of the sin of homogeneity, it would not be difficult for a prospective student or her family to reach that conclusion during the course of their college search. Similar language and images used to express similar purposes and outcomes. Small, sometimes trivial differences magnified to suggest distinction.

As Moon describes it, the sin of homogeneity is common, particularly in large and competitive industries. She describes a number of organizations and enterprises who have tackled the problem and succeeded in overcoming it, but I think the story of Apple Corporation's revival in the late 1990s provides particularly important insights about the power and value of a focused concentration on distinction.

Though the tale has by now taken on mythical proportions, it is clear that the Apple Corporation Steve Jobs inherited in his return as chief executive in 1997 was in deep trouble.[4] The company had struggled for a number of years by then, losing market share, losing investor confidence, and, most importantly, losing the interest and attention of the computer-buying public. By 1997, personal computers were on the cusp of ubiquity and the marketplace had become crowded with providers and choices. In a market that had been captured by Microsoft-based PCs, Apple products failed to stand out, or at least stand out to more than graphic designers and hardcore connoisseurs. Computers then did not offer the multidimensional range of functions they do today. Software was king. And in a sea of competitors selling a singular and largely undifferentiated product—often at lower price points—Apple was losing. From this was born "Think Different."

Among the first tasks Jobs took on in his return to Apple was to revive attention to the brand and separate it from its competitors on Apple's terms. He was not interested in creating separation simply on product features and attributes. ROM and RAM had already become commodities, and one computer looked and acted mostly like another. Those features by then had become table stakes. Instead, the "Think Different" campaign would focus on the power and value of creativity. More than a simple slogan, it was meant to define Apple Corporation, Apple products, and, perhaps most importantly, Apple users. It leveraged the emotional appeal that, though waning, had defined the Apple brand and separated it from its competitors throughout its history. The key was the use of the term "different." It was not meant to modify the verb "think" (as in "think differently," which would have been grammatically correct) but rather used as an abstract noun, which conveyed a much more powerful message: be different. A message easily translated into "be a leader," "be an innovator," "be creative," "be cool," "be great." Buy Apple.

The "Think Different" campaign didn't last long, but it reset the Apple brand and helped change its corporate trajectory. Aided by the subsequent launch of its iMac computer and the privatization of the Internet a year later, Apple succeeded beyond what could have been anyone's wildest expectations at the time. Today it is among the most successful and highly capitalized corporations in the world.[5]

Genomics, Part II

To limit the tale of Apple's resurrection to the particulars of a select industry or the creative choices of a remarkably imaginative CEO would miss the point entirely. Apple's story, and the "Think Different" brand campaign, points instead to the power and necessity of identifying and leveraging difference rather than similarity. The company chose to compete not only on features—features its products shared with most of its competitors—but also and more importantly on the explicit notion of being different (and, in their minds, interesting), a sentiment clearly valued then and now by consumers.

While the details of the story may be particular to Apple, the core lesson is important for higher education: in a crowded field of competitors providing an experience that shares many of the same features and attributes, the ability of a college or university to define a point of differentiation that creates value and is valued makes all the difference in the world. Rather than focusing our attention predominantly on what makes our institutions similar to each other, a practice common to rankings and peer analysis, we must instead dedicate much more energy to what makes us different, and therefore interesting or better in relation to our prospective students' other choices.[6]

Here, the language of genomics can be extended to provide a useful analogy. Humans share more than 80 percent of their genome with many species, including chimps (we all knew that), mice, cows, and dogs (it's likely not everyone knows that).[7] We share more than 99 percent of our genome with other human beings. That we share so much of the basic material of life with each other or with other creatures surely is fascinating, but what's really important is that the genetic material we don't share, whether it's 1 percent or 10 percent or 20 percent, defines us as individuals and makes each of us unique. It makes me, me and you, you.

Higher education shares much of the same structural story. Institutions of all types share a great deal of organizational DNA—in the form of mission, market, and management practices and values. At a broad institutional level, many of our missions read similarly, we have similar administrative structures, we approach markets similarly, we share financial practices and standards, we use similar administrative and programmatic decision-making rules and standards, we share similar ways of creating and counting credits, and we count success in similar ways. The list could go on. The same sorts of similarities also exist at the departmental level, where academic disciplines at all types of institutions often share similar structures and teaching methods, very often construct similar courses and curricular requirements (particularly at the lower division or introductory level), assign similar textbooks to their students, and approach grading similarly.

Clearly, significant differences exist among different types of institutions. Research universities, liberal arts colleges, and community colleges, for example, look, feel, and often operate in very different ways and often (though not always) serve different kinds of students. But within Carnegie Classification, each of those "species" of college or university most often is strikingly similar. That's not surprising. The classification system was created to organize postsecondary institutions based on the traits and characteristics they shared. Colleges and universities today frequently use the framework to anchor their identity and to identify and define their peers and competitors. Unfortunately, while the organizational model has great importance within higher education, very few prospective students and their families would describe themselves as connoisseurs of the nuanced institutional differences that undergird the Carnegie Classification system. Nor should they.

Here's the key point: if, say, 98 percent of our organizational DNA is shared with other peer and competitor institutions, then the 2 percentage points of difference need to make a difference. The distinction must be known;

it cannot be assumed or simply hoped for. It must be valued; there must be a market for it. It must be conveyed to the marketplace as valuable; we have to tell people why it matters. And it must ultimately deliver value; it must produce or yield what is pledged. A market defined by both intense competition and disruption demands an institutional commitment to distinction as a prerequisite for success. In those markets and under those circumstances, the ability to define and capture a comparative advantage becomes a leadership imperative, something like a search for the Holy Grail. And that's difficult work.

Reimagine Difference: Comparative Advantage

The first step required for building comparative advantage is *knowing* what programs, experiences, or attributes in fact make my institution distinctive. Amidst all that I do, what meaningfully sets me apart from my competitors and peers? Knowing those points of distinction and their value in more than superficial terms allows me to leverage the assets or market space I already own. If I cannot identify true points of distinction in my existing portfolio of programs and experiences, I must either choose where they could be developed or develop them from scratch, typically an expensive and time-consuming proposition. But in either case, distinction requires more than the ability to simply assert it. It rests on a commitment to knowing, understanding, and leveraging the market value of the distinction.

Comparative advantage requires understanding the difference between effectiveness and distinction and attributes and distinction. My institution may be good at many things. We may offer many programs and experiences, some that may not be available at other places. But we likely are distinctive or have a strong market position with only a few. The student calculation is simple: what about this college either is not available or is not available as well at another institution? An easy question to ask but more difficult for colleges and universities to answer. Colleges easily and often assert broad distinction. Features and attributes, sometimes outcomes, fill institutional web pages: "we prepare our graduates for career success," "we prepare ethical leaders," "ours is a diverse, dynamic community," "we are nationally recognized for excellence," "we nurture the whole student," "we prepare students to live lives of consequence."[8] Similar statements abound in the strategic plans of all types of colleges and universities. The list of claims could fill a book. Many of them are the same. Most are vague enough to be understood in a variety of ways. But what is less clear is how well these assertions are actually known or, more importantly, known as contemporary or sustainable sources of advantage, or even if they are true at all.

Several years ago while leading a planning discussion with the board of a Catholic secondary school, I asked the trustees if they believed families chose their school because it was Catholic or because it was a private alternative to public education. Those clearly were not mutually exclusive choices, but the school's Catholic identity was important to the board and I wanted to know how they understood it as a source of distinction and advantage. The majority indicated that they believed the school's Catholic identity was more important than its identity as a private school: they believed families chose the school *because* it was Catholic. That may once have been true, but their own data, which indicated that they enrolled a high percentage of non-Catholic students and were popular among families with a particular interest in the school's academic rigor, suggested it was no longer true, or as true, today. Was their Catholic identity distinctive? Surely, at least in relation to other schools that weren't Catholic. Did it confer to them a compelling source of market advantage? Much less clear and less likely. Rather than indicating what they knew, the directors instead asserted what they hoped for or felt. It is very easy to fall prey to well-intended hopes and wishes. Unfortunately, not knowing at all about true or real sources of distinction can have significant consequences. It can lead to program and image investments that miss the market and yield no positive gain, leaving institutional leaders and boards scratching their heads about what could have gone wrong.

The starting point for identifying a true distinctive space requires that college and university leaders resist the temptation to be all things to all people or, in the language of my native Lake Wobegon, the temptation to simply be "pretty good" at everything. It also requires a commitment to the kind of research that allows an institution to understand the value and value-added of the learning experiences it provides as well as research that allows it to understand why students chose it and how it compares to their next best choice.[9] In short, distinction and comparative advantage demand a continuous commitment to program evaluation and market research.

Students view distinction multilaterally, comparing one institution to another along any number of dimensions. They look around. They kick the tires. They compare. Then they choose. Points of distinction clearly appeal differently to different students. But well conceived and delivered, they can create compelling comparative advantages—or competitive space—that allow institutions to thrive in disruptive times.

Admission tactics by necessity are shaped by organizational needs and imperatives. Recruitment is built around the cycle of prospect-to-applicant-to-admit-to-matriculant. In a goal-oriented, deadline-driven process, we don't generally have time to reflect on the information or values or feelings that matter most at each stage of the selection process, or how students and families understand and experience us, or why students ultimately select us. Those questions often produce messy results, but understanding them provides a platform for shaping our experiences, our messages, and our student profile. In short, they help colleges and universities understand how they are valued.

The traditional admission funnel defines recruitment work flow and structure. It provides a useful method for organizing a complex and lengthy process. Admission offices need that structure to manage their time, resources, and energy. But the traditional funnel is a management tool, not a tool for understanding market behavior. To more fully understand the drivers influencing student choice, we need to focus on the needs and expectations that shape decision-making behavior throughout the process students and their families use to select a college. Doing so provides us with an opportunity to more clearly understand value and perceptions of value.

What would a market-focused admission process look like? The simplest way to conceive it is as an arrow that considers students' changing information needs and expectations at each step of the choice process.[10] The arrow concept defines temporal needs and expectations and provides colleges and

Discovery	Consideration	Selection
• Emotional	• Emotional	• Emotional
• Experiential	• Experiential	• Experiential
• Economic	• Economic	• Economic

The Enrollment Choice Arrow

universities with an opportunity to develop tactical recruitment plans to address them. The market arrow cannot replace the traditional admission funnel. But it can be employed as a supplement to it to focus our attention on market behavior and perceptions value.

The arrow model attempts to capture the broad elements of the college decision-making process. It rests on the notion that students and families come to their college choice in three stages, each stage building on the prior one.

1. *Discovery.* What are the *facts* about a particular college or set of colleges (including performance indicators like retention, graduation, and postcollege experience; location; majors and programs; admission requirements; cost and financial aid; etc.)? Students and parents compile their early information in a variety of ways, some of it controlled by colleges, like information provided on websites or through school visits, and much of it out of the direct control of colleges, like assessments found in proprietary guidebooks or gained in conversations they have with school guidance counselors or friends or parents. Students at this stage of their selection process seek general information from which they will later narrow their choices. The discovery stage often begins long before the students' senior year in high school and long before any institution's first formal contact with them.

2. *Consideration.* What *benefits* would I receive attending this college or university (a personal look at campus experiences and culture judged within the context of my aspiration)? In the consideration stage, students seek to narrow their broad set of choices to best choices. Understanding of return on investment—inclusive of intellectual investment, social investment, and financial investment—becomes a front-and-center need and expectation at this critical stage. Students and their parents want to know and understand the advantages and outcomes associated with particular institutions. Campus visits and personal interaction with staff, faculty, and students on campus, and alumni off campus become key shapers of value perceptions during the consideration stage.

3. *Selection.* Is this college or university the best *fit* for me in relation to my other choices (inclusive of my particular academic interests and expectations, my aspirations, my social needs and interests, and my family's economic situation)? The choice of a college ultimately becomes an expression of personal preference. Students try to match their sense of self with the experiences and opportunities provided by

a particular institution. It's an imperfect process, often fraught with anxiety and self-doubt (and sometimes self-deception). But the role and responsibility of the recruitment process should be to help students make a choice that will serve them best.

The horizontal stages of the model are defined by time and represent changing information needs as students hone in on a final choice. The vertical stages of the model focus on the multiple ways they define and experience value at each of those stages. Value comes in more flavors than vanilla. At each point of the college selection process, students and their families make judgments about value through not one but three distinct lenses:

1. *Emotional value.* What kinds of emotions do I feel when I step on campus? Are there people here who are like me? Will I fit in? Will my son or daughter grow as a person here? Will she or he feel safe and nurtured? Are the school's graduates happy? Do they speak enthusiastically about their college experience here? Admission professionals clearly understand the power of emotion in a student's choice, though my experience has been that too many colleges and universities do too little research to capture and quantify its role in the process. Unfortunately, outside of the admission office, emotional value too often is undervalued as a soft or intangible variable that stands apart from, or even detracts from, the educational and developmental mission of the institution. That kind of thinking is misplaced and vastly undersells the role of sensation in the selection process. Institutions need to care deeply about what and how students and families feel.

2. *Experiential value.* What kinds of opportunities will I have at this college? What kind of academic support and guidance will I receive? What is life like in the residence halls? How do students get involved in clubs and activities? Most campus energy is focused on experiential value, largely because we understand what we own and deliver. We want to believe that students choose us because of the constellation of opportunities we provide. We rightly take great pride in the curricular and cocurricular opportunities we offer. However, while those experiences clearly play a role in a student's college choice, there is great risk in overvaluing the size of that role in the final decision or in failing to understand whether they distinguish my institution in the marketplace. When the final choice is made, colleges and universities will be judged competitively.

3. *Economic value.* Where can this college take me in life? What doors will the experience open after college? Will I get a job? What do their alumni do for a living? What kinds of graduate schools could I attend? Is the net price of this school in line with what we can expect by way of eventual return? Is it worth it? Families today pay much more attention than ever to economic value and the financial return to a college education. They expect answers to their queries about return on investment. Institutions must be able to provide those answers in both quantitative and qualitative terms. We should be able to describe in more than superficial ways the employment experiences of our graduates as well as the value our alumni attach to having attended our institutions. Inability or unwillingness to provide that information leaves prospective students to speculate or to turn their attention to other institutions who are able to provide it.

Each of the parts of the market arrow is researchable and actionable. The framework presents opportunities for institutions to discover something deeper about their students and families—and then to do something about it. A long-time enrollment professional and colleague once said to me, "Every April I wake up in the middle of the night in a cold sweat thinking that my family eats because of the choices of 18-year-old boys and girls." A keen insight borne of experience.

Distinction and value together find their marketplace expression in comparative advantage. While it is important for colleges and universities to have an independent understanding of the value they create, that knowledge becomes most powerful when understood in terms of competitive advantage: what do we do better than our competition?

Prospective students today develop relationships with many institutions. They must decide what is important to them, how to evaluate the characteristics and opportunities presented to them, and then determine how those characteristics and opportunities compare among all of their choices. In the end, one choice is rated as better than all of the others. While that assessment of decision making is not particularly sophisticated, what's unusual is how infrequently colleges and universities gather and use the data necessary to understand it. Without the data and a commitment to use it, institutions are left to guess. And in a world of scarce resources, guessing is a dangerous game.

Colleges and universities ultimately must convey value along three important dimensions: academic or intellectual development, personal devel-

Campus Conversation Guide: Reimagine Difference

How are we understood by the students we seek to enroll as distinctive versus the other college choices they have?

What characteristics of the programs and experiences we provide do people describe as distinctive? Are our sources of distinction credible and relevant?

What are our primary sources of distinction and comparative advantage today versus our key competitors? Are those advantages unique to us or are they easily replicable? Are they sustainable?

Do we have the research or knowledge systems in place to define and capture distinction or understand comparative advantage?

What is the market footprint of our distinction? Among what types of students are we considered distinctive? Can we successfully and reliably meet our enrollment goals enrolling these kinds of students?

Is the market for our distinction large enough? Does it offer us enough growth opportunity to sustain us financially? If not, what are the alternatives?

opment, and professional or career development. Each dimension must be and can be supported by research. Each must reflect the experiences of current students as well as alumni. Perceptions of value are discoverable. And in the new marketplace for higher education, demonstrated value is king.

Reimagine Markets: Fit and Composition

Distinction and difference are prerequisites for success in competitive and disruptive markets. But a strong commitment to distinction will not, by itself, be sufficient to navigate disruptive market change. The changing demographic and economic characteristics of the traditional-age college population in America also demand careful thinking about how to best serve the next generation of students, whose needs and expectations may be quite different from those who preceded them.

Without doubt, remaining successful in current enrollment markets or succeeding in new ones requires a deep and broad understanding of who actually enrolls and succeeds at my institution and why they chose us. Our understanding must extend well beyond the dashboard profiles that fill books provided to trustees detailing the number, academic prowess, and geographic distribution of the new class. Important as that information may

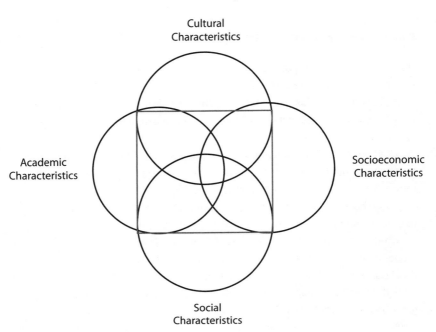

Cultural
Characteristics

Academic
Characteristics

Socioeconomic
Characteristics

Social
Characteristics

Student Characteristic Fit Map

seem, it rarely provides insights into the machinations of the marketplace or the factors that shape and drive student choice.

All students bring to college a bundle of characteristics and expectations. Taken altogether, those characteristics create a composite enrollment profile that can be summarized in a simple Venn diagram. Academic characteristics encapsulate the standard data typically collected and broadly shared: high school grade point averages, SAT or ACT test scores, and high school rank. But it also should include data reflecting academic motivation and aspiration: time spent on academic work in high school and expected in college, degree aspiration, parental educational attainment, self-assessment of academic ability and intellectual self-confidence, and any other information that provides insights into how students might engage their collegiate academic experiences.

Socioeconomic characteristics include family income, family wealth (which captures savings and other assets), the employment status of parents, and indicators of the importance of financial aid or net price to the final enrollment choice as well as the degree of difficulty the family expects in financing their son or daughter's college education. Because students often cannot accurately identify how much money their parents earn, financial aid applications provide the best source of income and wealth data. Irrespective of how the data are captured, it behooves an institution to compile the broadest picture possible of its student family income, wealth, and ability to pay.

Cultural and social characteristics are more wide ranging than either academic or socioeconomic characteristics but no less important. Cultural characteristics include, among other things, marital status of parents, where students come from (not only state, region, or country of residence but also urban, suburban, or rural residence), religious affiliation, race and ethnicity, and indicators of life values and priorities. Students do not arrive at institutions as blank slates. Their families, their communities, their experiences, and the beliefs and values they develop in their formative years shape who they are and how and with whom they identify themselves, which in turn influences how they will experience college.

Social characteristics reflect the developmental maturation of students. They suggest how students will engage their collegiate living experience and, more importantly, each other. Social characteristics and expectations can be captured by words or phrases students select to describe themselves, including terms like "outgoing," "friendly," and "shy"; their self-assessment of their social self-confidence in relation to their peers; and their college expectations for social engagement, including their expected level of participation in student activities as well as activities student development professionals wrestle with on a weekly basis, like drinking, partying, and gaming. Just as they are cultural beings when they arrive on campus, so too are students social beings. Social characteristics and expectations are particularly important to residential colleges and universities. They provide insights into the types of student activities and level of social support those institutions should provide. In addition, because they describe behavior and even social priorities, they provide early insights—perhaps even early warning—about life on campus.

Each of these characteristics—academic, socioeconomic, cultural, and social—overlap to paint a fuller picture of students than provided by the discrete and limited summaries typically prepared by colleges and universities for public consumption. The square in the center of the diagram is particularly important. It represents a kind of zone of similarity, the most common or intense expression of each of the four characteristic groups.

Most colleges and universities do not choose, and are not even able to choose, all of the characteristics that define their student body. They don't have access to enough advance information, nor do most generate the number of applications or have the brand standing or selectivity required to engineer a class at that level of precision. To twist a common analogy, if people are what they eat, then colleges are who they enroll. New markets are not born overnight. Over many years, the students we enroll define us more than we define them.

It also is true that students with particular characteristics and expectations are attracted to particular colleges or kinds of collegiate experiences. For example, the typical student at the College of Saint Benedict and Saint John's University is midwestern; from a two-parent, upper-middle-class, suburban Catholic family; academically strong and confident; and socially active, secure, and outgoing. They come to us with family values frequently described as traditional and, at least at the point of entry, they imagine those traditional values remaining part of their life after college. They deeply value and seek an experience of community. The quality of the social experience on campus is very important to them. These characteristics surely do not describe all of our students. But they describe the typical student—and taken altogether they attract students who share the same characteristics, values, and expectations.

Every college could compose a similar story to describe its students. To understand this more fully, take a college tour with a high school junior or senior to see what they see, listen to what they ask, and understand what they find most persuasive or even comfortable about the institution. Prospective students most similar to the current students they meet while touring campus are likely to be the most interested in the college. Their first personal connection with the college very often occurs when they meet their tour guide, typically a current student. In addition to learning about life on campus, they will almost always evaluate the tour guide and the other students they meet on the tour by asking themselves two simple questions: are these people like me and could they be my friends? Those are particularly important questions at residential colleges, where living communities are a key part of the experience. Though some students clearly select institutions intending to find difference, for others characteristic alignment and the comfort it offers will play a far larger role in the final decision, setting in motion a self-perpetuating "traditional" culture on campus. Like choosing like.

Changing the dominant culture on campus presents an extraordinary challenge. While colleges and universities often assert that they seek more difference in their student profile, in practice difference can be a very difficult goal to achieve. It forces prospective students to imagine what might be through the lens of what is, a difficult transition for anyone and an extraordinary expectation of an 18-year-old. The risk of difference, of being different, rests principally with the students themselves. What would it be like to be a Muslim student on a mostly Christian campus? What would it be like to be a student of color on a campus that is overwhelmingly white? What would it be like to be a GLBTQ student here? What would it be like to be a poor student on a campus filled with affluent students? Questions like these become very real and challenging for students who perceive themselves as living outside of the bounds of an institution's traditional or dominant student profile and culture. And they make it very difficult for an institution to change its student profile, or at least to change it quickly. Similar to their view of home as a geographic anchor, social and cultural familiarity also become anchors for students: few seek to stand out as social or cultural pioneers.

Difficult or not, though, the changing characteristics of the traditional college-age population will require colleges and universities to address these issues and to take active steps to mitigate or reduce the choice risk for students. College leaders must pay particular attention to students who do not share the dominant profile characteristics, taking steps to ensure that they have an experience that meets their needs and does not subject them to isolation in a sea of similarity. The burden of responsibility for meeting the needs of students—all students—rests with institutions, not with students, making a change in characteristic profile not simply a market proposition but also a mission proposition requiring an institutional examination of conscience. It is more important than ever today for college and university leaders to reimagine market strategies not only in relation to their enrollment and retention goals but also in relation to how they will effectively serve a new and different student body. Those twin considerations must be addressed simultaneously.

Reimagining markets also will require more active early market development through partnerships, consortia, and public policy leadership. My wife was for many years an elementary school teacher. More recently, she has served as a parent educator in our local school district's Early Childhood Family Education programs and as a parent educator for recent Hispanic immigrants. In a career working with children and their parents, she has experienced moments of great joy and hope as well as moments of tremendous frustration, and even sadness. She learned long ago that a child's future prospects most often are not shaped in high school but rather much earlier, often before they begin formal schooling. Her early childhood parent curriculum each year included a financial aid night to introduce families with very young children to college costs and to help them begin to prepare for college enrollment later. Though most don't realize it at the point their children are losing teeth or learning to ride a bicycle, eighteen years go by very quickly. Colleges and universities need to prepare similarly.

Colleges and universities have a significant role to play helping to create and shape the future pool of students. While postsecondary institutions cannot take on or replace the role of elementary and secondary schools, neither should they be bystanders to the early creation of college opportunity. The new demography—driven by students both less likely to come from families with a college experience and more likely to come from families with lower incomes—demands that we intervene in the college preparation process much earlier and more systematically than we have historically, either as individual institutions, through partnerships, or through public policy advocacy. Much is at stake for both students and colleges alike. We can play a wait-and-see game, gambling that enough high school students will meet our standards for preparation, readiness, and potential, or we can take more assertive preemptive steps designed to improve their readiness and preparation beginning at a much earlier age. In a changing marketplace, early action is the wiser approach. How much and how well we work with middle and secondary schools and their students, as well as even younger students, has broad social, economic, and enrollment implications.

The formal college recruitment process today at most institutions begins as early as the 10th grade, when colleges and universities send out their first admission marketing pieces. The process intensifies over the next twenty-four to thirty-six months as postal mail boxes and email inboxes of prospective students fill to their capacity and beyond. As students apply to college, colleges examine their high school records and board scores with the same intensity an avid baseball fan reads a box score. We comb through their essays and personal statements, trying in a very short period of time to gauge preparation, readiness, potential, and fit. All colleges and universities dream or fantasize about large and fully qualified applicant pools.

But the act of selecting a college begins long before the first search mailing or the first colorful brochures arrive in the mail. In a 2010 study sponsored by the Minnesota Private College Research Foundation, only 11 percent of all parents of middle school students in Minnesota described middle school as too early to start planning for college.[11] More than half said it was *too late*. The research also found that many middle school parents had already begun to form college preferences for their children. But more than anything else, parents of pre-high-school-age children craved reassurance. They wanted help identifying ways to save for college and with preparing their children for college.

As someone who spent a considerable amount of time in birthing centers awaiting the arrival of each of my four children, I believe that even middle school seems like a long time to wait to begin thinking about college. While parents of infants and toddlers do not need information about particular colleges and universities—tempting as it may be to begin shaping institutional preferences that early—we can begin then to inform them about the value of college, the need to plan academically and financially for college, and the steps they should consider as their children progress through elementary and secondary school. The sooner we reach young families, the more time they will have to prepare academically, financially, and emotionally, which can expand their college choices and improve their readiness when we fully engage them years later as prospective students.

Enrollment in college is preceded by five mostly sequential and easy-to-remember steps. Students must be *aware* of college, they must *aspire* to college, they must have reached some level of *achievement* to get into a college, they must *apply* to at least one college, and they ultimately must be able to *afford* the college to which they are admitted. Enrollment cannot happen until all five steps have been fulfilled. Though the vast majority of college recruitment effort focuses on the last two steps of the process, the first three define and shape the marketplace. And for first-generation students, those whose parents have no college experience, the first three steps can be every bit as foreboding and daunting as the last two.

Real college opportunity requires real college preparation. However, as more students go to college, it has become clear that a significant, sometimes very high percentage of them do not enroll academically well prepared for success in college. Just two-thirds of all high school graduates in the country met the ACT organization's College Readiness Benchmarks in English in 2012.[12] Worse, only 52 percent met the reading benchmark, 46 percent the mathematics benchmark, and a dismal 31 percent the science benchmark. Only one-quarter met or surpassed the benchmarks in all four subject areas. Nearly 3 in 10 test-taking high school graduates reached none of the college readiness benchmarks. The College Board reported similar results among SAT test takers: 57 percent of all test takers in the class of 2012 failed to meet the SAT's College and Career Readiness Benchmark.[13] Neither result is at all encouraging, as legions of unprepared students head to college each fall.

Lack of college preparation is a particularly significant problem among lower-income students, many of whom begin postsecondary careers at a serious academic disadvantage vis-à-vis their peers from families with higher incomes. According to ACT, Inc., in the seven states where all 11th graders took the ACT test in 2012, only 45 percent of students from low-income families met the English benchmark standard, 30 percent the reading benchmark, 21 percent the mathematics benchmark, and just 13 percent the science benchmark.[14] If those scores are at all predictive, they suggest that the majority of lower-income students will struggle mightily at most colleges and universities in the United States.

As elementary school teachers know best of all, educational disadvantage often begins at early grade levels and becomes much harder to redress later. In their 2013 report on college readiness, ACT, Inc. noted that "students who were far off-track in eighth grade had only a 10 percent chance in reading, 6 percent chance in science, and 3 percent chance in mathematics of reaching ACT's College Readiness Benchmarks by twelfth grade. In higher poverty schools, those numbers were 6 percent, 3 percent and 3 percent." In other words, for the vast majority of students who find themselves academically out of sync as early as middle school, the readiness die appears cast. Their chances of making up ground already lost appear slim, particularly for low-income students. ACT stressed the need to keep students on track academically in early grades, long before they reach middle school and high school. That's very good advice. Early investments in achievement can reduce the need for more difficult remediation later. From the vantage point of colleges and universities, remedial education is already a large, resource-intensive enterprise. Three-quarters of all public four-year colleges and universities, 60 percent of private four-year institutions, and nearly all public two-year institutions already offer remedial instructional courses and support programs designed for students who lack the curricular competencies required to succeed in college.[15] Better preparation could free those resources for use in support of academic achievement and curricular improvement.

Poor college readiness represents an extraordinary drain of human capital and a threat to college and university enrollment prospects. Stage-by-stage losses conspire to reduce educational progress from a pipeline to something more like a straw—and a highly selective straw at that, one that favors and benefits most students from families with the highest incomes. For reasons of both social interest and self-interest, college and university leaders cannot sustain high and early loss rates in the new demographic era. Independently and collectively, colleges and universities need to take concerted steps to ensure a more effective and productive educational pipeline, particularly at important transition points in the educational process. That will require institutions to allocate more of their own resources toward what can best be described as market development—programs and activities designed to improve awareness, aspiration, and achievement at earlier ages. Most colleges already sponsor outreach or readiness programs of one sort or another, often under the auspices of public service or service learning and very often in partnership with other community-based educational organizations. However, looking forward at the scale of market change in front of us, it's important that we ensure that our developmental work is integrated and not fragmented within the bounds of operational silos. Our ability to

---

Campus Conversation Guide: Reimagine Markets

Can we continue to rely on the types of students we currently enroll or whom we have traditionally enrolled to meet our class goals?

Do we have a strong and sustainable market position among the students we seek to enroll? How much of our demand is real and how much is illusory or not serious?

Should we, or must we, seek new and/or different students than we have traditionally enrolled?

How will we define and identify those students?

What programs and experiences do we offer or must we offer that will appeal to them?

Do we have the relationships or partnerships in place to build sustainable markets for the future?

How will we serve a changing mix of new and traditional students to best meet their needs and expectations?

Are we prepared academically, socially, and culturally to meet the needs of students who are new to our campus and to our campus culture? What must we change? Are these changes aligned with our mission and our core competencies?

more fully integrate those activities will improve our ability to develop and serve prospective and then enrolled students.

Reimagine Management: Finding a New Fiscal Equilibrium

The new market for higher education requires college and university leaders to commit more assertively to comparative advantage and market development. But those commitments alone will not amount to enough at most institutions without a similar commitment to a new and more sustainable fiscal future. The central issues facing colleges and universities across the country today are economic—threatening a potentially devastating imbalance between revenues, expenditures, and perceptions and expectations of value. Can we reliably generate the revenue necessary to support the collegiate experience we seek to deliver? While conversations about fiscal equilibrium may not generate the creative energy associated with comparative advantage and market development, they will be every bit as important and necessary in coming years.

Changing economic characteristics of new students (a higher proportion of whom will be the first in their family to go to college), real economic constraints for all types of families, rapidly rising public skepticism about the ability of colleges and universities to economically manage themselves, and mounting pressure for new and lower-cost forms of higher education have disrupted the fiscal landscape for many institutions. Extraordinary pressure to reduce or more effectively manage both the price and cost of college will define the foreseeable future. No amount of wishful thinking about economic growth and a return to halcyon days gone by will change that basic reality for most institutions. How much should a quality college education cost? How should it be priced? Are the relationships of price, cost, and value clear or even partly clear? Answers to those questions are important. And responses like "more," "less," or "we don't know" provide no guidance for decision making.

I began my career as a budget analyst for the State of Minnesota. I quickly learned that budget decision making mostly boiled down to the management of constraints. Those constraints could be encapsulated in a simple two-by-two matrix: revenue constraints and expense constraints on one axis, and absolute constraints (those required or imposed by an outside condition) and conditional constraints (those that are self-imposed or chosen) on the other axis. The same basic forces also shape budget decision making at colleges and universities. Revenue is always finite. Demand for spending most often seems infinite. In that context, how can scarce resources be allocated to derive the greatest possible outcome (however "outcome" is described, a particularly vexing issue in higher education)? How can we strike a working balance of constraints and aspiration in support of the highest-quality experience we can deliver?

More than thirty years after it was first published, economist Howard Bowen's Revenue Theory of Cost continues to provide important insights about the relationship of revenues and expenditures in postsecondary education. Bowen's theory asserted that "[at] any given time, the unit cost of education is determined by the amount of revenues currently available for education relative to enrollment. The statement is more than a tautology, as it expresses the fundamental fact that unit cost (i.e., the cost of education) is determined by hard dollars of revenue and only indirectly by considerations of need, technology, efficiency, and market wages and prices."[16]

In practice, the theory could be described thus: institutions raise as much money as they can and spend as much money as they raise. Bowen posited that differences in spending among different colleges and universities could be explained principally by differences in their ability to raise revenue. Though his writing preceded the contemporary fascination with rankings, most best-of lists ultimately reward institutions with the most resources: the colleges and universities who have the most money generally spend the most per student and garner the highest reputations. The incentive is clear. Raising more money to be able to spend more money has a reputational payoff in the marketplace, independent of how well the money is spent. In Bowen's model, revenue opportunity acts as the primary constraint or brake on spending. And for that reason, revenue growth strategies typically are regarded as preferable to expense management strategies in higher education, at least as a lead step in budget decision making. In many ways, Bowen's theory also could describe household spending in America: more income provides greater opportunity for more spending, often independent of clearly defined needs.

The problem, though, is immediately clear. The decision-making behavior associated with the Revenue Theory of Cost sets in motion a never-ending money chase that at some point may become unsustainable when revenue can no longer be raised quickly enough to support growing expense needs and wants. Beyond ordinary annual income, accumulated wealth ultimately is required to continue playing the game successfully, and few colleges and universities in America are wealthy (or wealthy enough to sustain themselves independent of other revenue pressures). In 2012, one-quarter of the more than 800 endowment funds reported to the National Association of College and University Business Officers by US higher education institutions, systems, and foundations reported endowed resources of $36 million or less. Half reported values below $85 million.[17] Ten private universities in the United States today hold more than 40 percent of the total endowment assets of all private colleges and universities in the country. Similarly, just ten public universities hold one-third of the total endowment assets of all public institutions in the country.[18] Most institutions neither began nor ended the Great Recession with significant wealth. And most will never become wealthy.

Absent extraordinary wealth or wealth potential, other market-driven sources of annual revenue—like net tuition from students and families or taxpayer appropriations—become more important. When the broad economy grows, as it did for years prior to the Great Recession, market-based revenue strategies work well. But when economic growth slows or stops, the strategy no longer works as well. Market-based revenue constraints today are more challenging than they have been at any point in the last two decades. Flat or falling family income has limited the ability of many colleges and universities to raise net tuition revenue, an extraordinary constraint for tuition-dependent institutions. Slow economic growth, coupled with changing social needs and priorities, has resulted in sometimes precipitous reductions in state support for public colleges and universities. The rapid rise in the stock market since the depths of the Great Recession has offset some of the losses in net tuition or state appropriations, but investment gains have mostly favored the already wealthy. Large percentage growth on a small investment portfolio is nice, but can't compare to large percentage growth on a large investment portfolio. The math virtually ensures widening gaps between already rich institutions and everyone else. Economic disruption, then, compels us to think differently. It requires a recalibration of fiscal equilibrium that addresses new and likely long-lasting fiscal constraints. And that must begin with a realistic assessment on both the revenue and expense side of the budget ledger.

Pricing

Conversations about college affordability today too often begin and end with the pre–financial aid sticker price of attendance. Occasionally, in an attempt to add at least some sophistication to the discussion, they include the average price of attendance across all students after the receipt of grants and scholarships. However, neither of those data points alone is particularly helpful, either to families or to college leaders, because neither conveys enough information about affordability or institutional price strategy and neither effectively links the price of attendance with the cost of providing the experience.

Families and the broader public often misunderstand the sticker price of college, viewing it as *the* price. They increasingly express outrage at colleges' desire to continuously raise it without end and wonder how the cost of education could have gotten so high. Complicating the discussion, the leap from sticker price to highly differentiated net price is neither intuitive nor simple for most people, particularly for students who come from families with no prior experience of college, but even for those from families with college experience who do not take the time to understand the availability of merit-based scholarship aid. The headlines in the popular media are not at all helpful, by and large suggesting that the price of college has risen beyond the grasp of most families.

As highly differentiated net pricing has become the dominant practice at most colleges and universities, the sticker price of attendance conveys less information than ever before about the real cost or value of college. By 2010, only one-third of all first-time, full-time undergraduate students attending public four-year colleges and universities nationally, and just 1 in 6 students enrolled at private four-year institutions, were paying the full price of attendance, meaning they received no grant or scholarship assistance.[19] The vast majority of their peers received a price discount of one kind or another—based on ability to pay, academic or personal characteristics, or some combination of both. For most students and families, the posted total price is little more than a starting point, rarely an end, which has the effect of decoupling the net price they pay from the real cost of providing the learning experience and the value they receive from it.

All colleges and universities today bend price curves, increasingly like a pretzel. Net price strategy most often is highly customized to the characteristics of individual students. Students pay all manner of prices dependent on the characteristics, financial and nonfinancial, that they present at the point of application, rendering financial aid a kind of boutique interchange. When asked whether the market can bear the price we charge, we can truthfully respond only in relation to the sometimes vast collection of net prices our students actually pay. Almost no private college or university in the country, and virtually none of the public flagship universities, now lives at a posted sticker price that could reasonably be considered "affordable" to even half of the general population in the country without financial assistance of some kind. We price differentially from a fixed starting point because it allows us to meet individual students where they are while at the same time affording us the opportunity to generate the revenue necessary to provide a particular kind of learning experience. The only singular price point that universally serves all students is zero, an obviously unworkable response to demands for affordability. However, appropriately set in relation to its markets, the sticker price of attendance can provide a college or university with an opportunity to meet both its enrollment and net revenue goals. Inappropriately set, it fails on both counts.

In the end, price strategy is both a financial exercise and a value exercise. High or low price points for an experience that ultimately cannot deliver more than superficial value to students will be subject to the ruin of market skepticism. Just as high price carries the risk of market deselection, so too does low price if it cannot deliver what a student expects. Irrespective of the

---

Campus Conversation Guide: Reimagine Pricing

How does our price strategy enable us to enroll the kinds of students we seek? How do we use discounting strategy to achieve our broad enrollment goals?

Does our volume of demand, as indicated by applications for admission, provide us with real pricing power?

How does our sticker price and net price compare to our key competitors? Do we have a value advantage that provides us with pricing power?

With what kinds of students does our pricing strategy work best and with whom least well? How are those markets changing?

What role does net price play in our students' decision to choose us? How important is financial aid to their final college choice?

Do we have a compelling and transparent narrative that links price to value? Is that narrative readily understood by trustees, administrative leadership, and faculty?

Does our price strategy generate the net revenue required to support the learning experience we provide or wish to provide? Can the strategy generate sustainable revenue as both our markets and our learning experiences change?

net price students must pay to attend a particular college, the institution must deliver an experience that they value in some way. In economic terms, the value of the learning experience must equal or exceed the financial effort required by a student or family to pay for it. It's quite clear that families of all means will stretch to pay for college (many of them a great deal) if they believe the experience is worth it. Is there a singular price point at which the market will reject us in total and out of hand? Not likely. There are hundreds. That's why colleges and universities must continuously attend to the pulse and needs of the markets in which they swim. Markets generally don't fail. Strategies do.

Spending

The lingering effects of slow economic growth coupled with changing demography clearly indicate that robust and sustainable gains in net tuition revenue will remain a challenge throughout the foreseeable future. Even if the sticker price of tuition rises at a slower rate than it has in the last two decades, most colleges and universities, public and private, still can expect significant demand for financial assistance from students and families of all types, which will have a dampening effect on growth in tuition income.

Tuition-dependent institutions (who comprise the vast majority of private colleges and universities) will, of course, feel the effects of market change and slow revenue growth most quickly and most fully. In an effort to reduce their reliance on tuition and minimize their exposure to market change and pressure, those institutions surely will redouble their efforts to raise money from nontuition sources. It likely will take years to derive the payoff of those strategies, and the changes typically will be experienced in small, not large, increments. Imagine a college that enrolls 2,000 students on an annual operating budget of $60 million, where 75 percent of the revenue is derived from student tuition. An endowment gift to the college of $10 million—an extraordinary gift by any definition, particularly to a small college—typically would generate just $500,000 in new annual operating income. It would reduce tuition dependency by less than 1 percentage point. A 5-percentage-point reduction in tuition dependency would require $3 million in new resources, equivalent to a 20 percent increase in nontuition revenue at our mythical college and a stiff challenge for most institutions. Most wealthy institutions have been members of their own rarified club for a long time. Far fewer have accumulated the resources required to join them.

The constraints imposed by slowly rising net tuition revenue, coupled with fund-raising realities and, for public institutions, reduced taxpayer support, will require most colleges and universities to turn more assertively to the expense side of the budget ledger to manage their fiscal equilibrium. Few institutions will have the good fortune to address the demands and challenges of the new marketplace solely through revenue growth. No colleges or universities, particularly those without significant institutional wealth, can sustain a long-term imbalance between their revenue realities and their operational ambitions. At the end of the day, operations must be in sync with aspirations. If poorly aligned, one or both must be altered to strike a new balance. And that most often will require a hard look at ways to manage expenses and expense growth.

Colleges and universities almost always find expense-side management difficult. It too frequently gets reduced to headline terms like "just reduce administration" or "eliminate the frills" or "become more efficient." But those overly simplified and highly valenced demands mean vastly different things to different people. Do we mean that administration writ large creates no value? What exactly makes something a frill and for whom? What trade-offs in effectiveness may be required to become more efficient? Anyone in a leadership role at a college or university knows how vexing those choices and trade-offs can be, particularly when they conflict with our institutional DNA.

While attending a conference a number of years ago, I listened to the president of a flagship university describe a lengthy letter he had received from a distinguished faculty member suggesting detailed improvements and efficiencies in a variety of academic departments and disciplines. Except in his own. When the president responded to the faculty member, thanking him for offering his ideas for consideration, he asked, what about your department? The response he received was swift and brief: my department is fine. A funny story well told, but also revelatory. Efficiency is someone else's problem, not mine, a variation of George Carlin's comedy routine, "my stuff is stuff, your stuff is junk."

Nearly all programs and activities have constituencies who view them as valuable, even essential, particularly in service industries like higher education, which makes it extraordinarily difficult to effect meaningful or swift change, and sometimes even small change. In 2010, the College of Saint Benedict and Saint John's University eliminated Nordic skiing as a varsity-level sport—consigning it instead to club sport status. Very few colleges in

Minnesota any longer offered varsity Nordic skiing. More importantly, moving the program to club status freed resources (travel and some coaching) that could be reallocated to other high-demand club sport activities. Though the change did not generate anything close to a resource windfall, the reallocated funds would benefit a larger number of students in other club sports. But it clearly did not benefit the two dozen students who were part of the varsity Nordic ski team. They were understandably hurt and angry and turned to social media to express their displeasure. Soon, letters poured in from Nordic skiers across the country and even the globe, most of whom likely had never heard of us prior to that point, decrying the change and demanding a revocation of the decision.

In the end, we did not reinstate Nordic skiing as a varsity sport. The experience, however, provided a useful lesson, one drawn from political circles. Change, real or threatened, results in mobilization of constituent groups who very often cast the action in deeply personal terms. As a result, change on campus can take on a *Horton Hears a Who* quality—a change is a change no matter how small (and to those immediately impacted, change almost never seems small). It may be difficult to initially create a program or activity, but once created and woven into our institutional fabric those programs and activities are difficult to alter or remove, particularly when they are perceived as vital to our mission, to our experience, or to our community. The more sweeping the change, or the more a change conflicts with historic values and practices, the more difficult it will be to accomplish.

Three other conditions, none wholly unique to higher education but key parts of the DNA of most traditional colleges and universities, also complicate spending choices:

1. Much of our labor force—and our entire faculty—is built around highly specialized knowledge and skills not easily transferrable to other activities. I may be oversubscribed in biology and undersubscribed in modern and classical languages, but I cannot move my excess capacity from one to the other. Similarly, my financial aid professionals are not also prepared to be effective academic advisors or information technology specialists. Traditional and deeply valued practices like tenure—which represents a long-term and stable commitment to high-quality teaching and research—have the effect of broadening our fixed costs and limiting short-term budget options. More broadly, most colleges and universities are vertically organized, each division

employing professionals with a focused skill set. Specialization creates value because it brings expert knowledge to campus, in the classroom and the lab as well as in administrative offices. At the same time, though, a highly specialized workforce and divisional structure makes it more difficult to easily or rapidly adapt to changing needs, demands, and conditions. People, most of them highly educated and trained, are the primary asset at colleges and universities.[20] Human resource spending typically represents the largest cost on our financial statements. It's no surprise, then, that labor force choices most often present our most challenging budget choices.

2. Though the image of college and university management as a kind of collegium is more myth than reality in contemporary higher education, neither are most public and nonprofit institutions today organized as linear command-and-control enterprises. Higher education historically has valued deliberation and collegiality, community and consultation, even when, and perhaps especially when, it slows decision-making processes to ensure the consideration of more voices. The collaborative, sometimes hyperdemocratic style of management that characterizes American higher education has on balance served students and institutions very well over hundreds of years, ensuring that institutional values receive due consideration and deliberation. At the same time, though, it also can create an insular protect-at-all-cost inertia that clouds leadership's ability to react to change or opportunity with dispatch or conviction.

3. Unlike a manufacturing industry, which can readily measure and evaluate outputs per unit of input, higher education has a much less certain production function. Colleges and universities often struggle with ideas of efficiency and effectiveness because they lack well-understood or definitive metrics for evaluating either. While inputs are reasonably simple to measure—they fill the pages of college guidebooks—educational and developmental outputs are much more difficult to assess and interpret. It is easy to measure degree completion. It is much more difficult to describe and subsequently measure what constitutes an educated person. Moreover, there is not a singular formula or algorithm that shapes the relationship between units of educational input and a particular output or outcome. How many people does it take to educate a student? How many hours of study are required to prepare a student for a career after college? We do not have reliable or universal benchmark

standards for these kinds of questions, not least of all because the outputs and outcomes are so dependent on the behavior and engagement of the people—students, faculty, and staff—who comprise the inputs. The uncertain relationship between inputs and outputs in higher education vastly complicates decision making and expense management, making it much more difficult to evaluate the effect of any particular change.

None of these considerations provides institutional leaders with a free pass from making difficult decisions. Organizations of all types must make hard choices, often with only a vague or hopeful sense of the outcome. The urgency for making difficult spending choices in higher education surely is rising as the market changes, its expectations for performance change, and internal and external financial pressures increase. However, as we deliberate and consider our options, we must acknowledge these particular and peculiar issues, each wrapped in our organizational DNA, as part of our decision-making milieu. They shape and influence our decision-making motivation as well as the quality and character of our choices.

As institutional resources become more constrained, the need to balance pressures for efficiency with imperatives for effectiveness will come into sharper focus, requiring a working understanding of trade-offs. Think of it much like you would cause and effect: this gain in efficiency comes at this price. Changing the faculty and staff computer replacement cycle from four years to six years, for example, may save a certain amount of money, but it may also result in diminished workforce productivity in the later years of the cycle. Similarly, increasing the student-to-faculty ratio from 12:1 to 14:1 may generate significant budget savings, but depending on how it is achieved, it may also reduce student-faculty contact central to the learning experience or to the institutional brand. Choices like these, required or not, should always be made with eyes wide open. Efficiency and effectiveness play out as two sides of the same coin, related and interdependent. Understanding their relationship is key to sound budget decision making.

Sustained economic disruption will make value-challenging expense choices unavoidable for most colleges and universities. Few will be spared. The choices will become even more difficult, and the choice set even more limited, in the coming years if we allow the already demanding issues in front of us to fester unattended. How institutional leaders approach and frame their choices will matter as much as the particular choices they make.

Campus Conversation Guide: Reimagine Spending

What key constraints, existing or emerging, are reshaping our budget? Are there opportunities available that could change the nature or effect of those constraints?

Are our revenues and expenditures sustainably balanced? Can each continue to grow at rates that ensure balance in the future?

Are the curricular and cocurricular programs and activities we currently provide financially sustainable in the context of changing student needs and expectations and our revenue model?

What level of service or quality can we maximally provide within the resources we have available?

What operational choices or trade-offs are required to achieve our strategic aspirations?

What spending choices have we defined as nonnegotiable in relation to our mission or values? What choices are nonnegotiable in relation to our institutional brand or comparative advantage? Can we afford to continue to define these choices as nonnegotiable?

How do we understand and define value when making spending decisions? What tools do we have in place for understanding and measuring the relationship of spending and value-added?

Integrative Thinking

Pricing and spending, more versus less, this choice or that choice. Effective decision making ultimately rests on strong integrative decision-making skills. Seemingly simple questions—like how many students we should enroll, what student profile we should seek, or what programs we should offer or enhance—are much more complex than they appear at first blush. They encompass many variables, dependent, independent, and interdependent, and weave together all manner of student and market characteristics as well as the learning identity an institution projects to the marketplace.

Effective action demands that the multiple choice variables be dimensionalized in ways that clarify their points of intersection and highlight required trade-offs.[21] A choice made along any single market, mission, or management dimension always has consequences for the other dimensions. For example, a decision to increase undergraduate enrollment, simple and common enough, also requires reflection on enrollment profile and educational identity. What will happen to our profile when we choose to enroll more students? Who will comprise the increment? What kind of net tuition will they generate? Is our current educational identity appealing enough to attract the additional students we seek to enroll? Do we have the brand horsepower to achieve and sustain larger enrollment? Do we have the support services and physical capacity to serve a larger student body? Those questions require careful thought, but the overarching point is quite simple: there are no wholly independent or discrete choices. Instead, all market-related choices must be considered through an integrative lens, an exercise in horizontal, not vertical, thinking. During disruptive times, it is particularly important that college and university leaders have a well-formed and well-informed sense of those interactions. The institution's future will depend on it. Think different.

CHAPTER NINE

Breakpoint

He is the best man who, when making his plans, fears and reflects on everything that can happen to him, but in the moment of action is bold.

—Herodotus (Greek Historian, c. 484–424 BC)

At the heart of business success is the ability to compete; the ability to compete, in turn, is dependent on the ability to differentiate from competitors.

—Youngme Moon, *Different*

Mobiles are fascinating art objects not just because they are beautiful and elegant but because they force the observer to reflect on concepts of equilibrium and balance. Absent equilibrium, a mobile is nothing more than a pile of unrelated and uninteresting material. Equilibrium is a powerful economic concept, as well, representing a point of optimal efficiency, effectiveness, and productivity. In periods of market change and shifting preferences, finding a point of equilibrium becomes an especially difficult task. Disequilibrium creates discomfort and instability, neither a desirable position for organizations nor the markets they serve. However, it also can create opportunity. And therein lies the challenge: finding opportunity during disequilibrium.

The new and still evolving marketplace for higher education—characterized by changing demographics, changing economics, and changing cultural expectations—demands a recalibration of equilibrium on campus. Most colleges and universities will need to find a new point of sustainable mission, market, and management balance, the point at which their operations are secure enough to create intermediate or longer-term prospects for the achievement of their aspirations. Phrased more simply as a question: what steps must institutions take to create sustainable conditions for excellence in the context of a shifting marketplace that demands continuous adaptation? For their part, in the wake of the Great Recession and the new economic realities it spawned, students and families also will seek a new point of equilibrium, striking a balance between what they are able to pay (an economic question) and what they are willing to pay (a value question) for college. Each point of equilibrium, institutional and familial, will result from a complex set of decisions wholly owned by neither institutions nor families.

Mission, market, and management choices should not be by-products of neglect or drift. Few colleges and universities today can afford the cost and consequences of either. It will take decisive, determined, and thoughtful leadership to address the challenges and choices we face in the coming years, but there simply is no alternative. Reflecting the extraordinary diversity of American higher education, each institution will have to find its own way.

I recommend Steven Levitt and Stephen Dubner's wonderful book *Freakonomics* to students and friends. Levitt and Dubner provide entertaining and insightful lessons on the values of curiosity and paying attention. The sometimes freakish economics of higher education today, driven by demographic, market, and cultural forces, also require our full attention. That there are no easy or readily apparent solutions to the choices and challenges in front of institutional leaders makes their commitment to addressing them that much more important. We must address complex choices, as must our students and their families. It will be impossible to please everyone as those difficult choices are made. Still, the changing conditions reshaping the world of higher education in America should lead us neither to gloom nor to despair but rather to the pursuit of opportunity and advantage. With a better understanding of the forces at play in the world around us and a more complete understanding of our own place in that world, we can make institutional choices that advance our values and serve students and the common good for generations to come.

ACKNOWLEDGMENTS

This book has been more than twenty years in the making. It reflects the collective insights, guidance, and wisdom of friends, colleagues, and mentors from around the country. I am fortunate and blessed to have had the opportunity to learn so much from so many smart, interesting, and wonderful people.

Two presidential transitions occurred at my institutions as I was writing. I would like to express my deep gratitude to MaryAnn Baenninger and Mary Hinton, presidents of the College of Saint Benedict, and Robert Koopmann, OSB, and Michael Hemesath, presidents of Saint John's University, who offered me both the leave time to write as well as the encouragement to put these ideas together and express them. I have benefited greatly from their generosity and wisdom. I also have been fortunate over many years to work with extraordinary cabinet colleagues. This book reflects their acumen and insights.

Ernie Diedrich taught my first college economics course in fall 1980. I was a first-year undergraduate student and he a new professor. That introductory microeconomics course opened up a new world of ideas to me that I have never forgotten. He encouraged and cajoled me to write this book years ago. I finally took his advice and thank him for his inspiration, friendship, and mentorship.

David B. Laird, Jr., past president of the Minnesota Private College Council, was my most critical reader and my greatest professional friend and mentor. In 1992, when I began a new position as vice president for research at the Council, he challenged me to look at the broad trends impacting higher education and to think outside of traditional boxes for ways to describe and address them. Over many years we often have had spirited discussions, sometimes spirited disagreements, but have always landed in the same place: American higher education is a treasure that must be preserved and nurtured.

David's deep passion for extending education opportunity to those for whom it historically has not been available has shaped and influenced both my professional thinking and my personal commitments.

Over his more-than-four-decade career, Cal Mosley has forgotten more about college admissions and the key trends impacting colleges and universities than I will ever know. He has throughout his long professional life remained a keen student of higher education. He brings a special wisdom and infectious enthusiasm to his work. I shared with him every chapter I wrote as I completed them and am deeply grateful for the insights he offered to improve the narrative. He is a gifted leader in college admission and a great friend.

I thank Kathy Parker and the entire staff of the CSB/SJU libraries for providing me with an ever-so-monastic private study in which to write at the Alcuin Library at Saint John's University. As the parent of four school-age children, I quickly learned that writing at home would not be a workable option. I am particularly grateful for the assistance of Bev Ehresmann, who graciously rescued me more than once when I found myself in the library but locked out of my writing room.

This narrative would not have come together without the opportunities provided by Hardwick Day and The Lawlor Group to develop and introduce many of these themes. I am deeply grateful to John Lawlor and Jim Day for the many occasions they have provided me over the years to express ideas and explore trends, often using their clients as test markets. They do extraordinary work in and for higher education and are among the finest trend watchers I know.

Dan Nelson, Chris Farrell, Richard Cook, David Laird, Leo Munson, Fred Senn, Paul Cerkvenik, Jose Peris, Jim Lande, Michael Hemesath, and Mary Hinton served as critical readers of the manuscript. They used their valuable time to provide important critiques that greatly improved the final text. I owe them a great debt of gratitude. Mark Geller of High Impact Training in St. Cloud, Minnesota, has been an extraordinary advocate for me and these ideas. He also persistently reminded me that I needed to finish the book. Greg Britton at Johns Hopkins University Press provided wise and gentle guidance as he helped me navigate the publishing process. Thank you!

For the wisdom and extraordinary patience they have provided me over many years, I thank Joe Russo, Dan Saracino, Dick Bellows, Tom Willoughby, Anne Sturtevant, Ken Jones, Bill Hall, Mary Milbert, Dan Nelson, Martha Pitts, Kevin Menk, Mary Nucciarone, Ken Redd, Heather

McDonnell, Leo Munson, Steve DesJardins, Marla Friederichs, Mark Lindenmeyer, Chris Farrell, Michael Kyle, Katie Johnson, Fred Senn, Jack Rayburn, Terry Lahti, Owen Sammelson, Brian Zucker, Pam Horne, Scott Friedhoff, Rod Oto, Shelly Regan, Jon Boeckenstedt, Nathan Mueller, Gary McVey, and John Olson. I hope they see their insights expressed in this book.

I have been on a bowling team for more than a decade. I'm not a particularly good bowler, though my handicap score occasionally helps us out in Tuesday night league play. I want to thank the members of my team—Ed Voight, Rob Klein, Rick Halloran, Jay Kraus, and Jeff Holthaus—for providing me with important, and almost always colorful, insights into Main Street America and the concerns and issues of real families. Ed's daughter enrolled at the College of Saint Benedict in fall 2013. I learned much from him and the questions he asked throughout his daughter's college search process.

I am deeply grateful for the editorial assistance of Andrea McGee, my sister-in-law. She copy edited the initial manuscript and helped improve the flow and readability of the narrative. She and my brother Brian also generously allowed me to share their story about the challenge of family saving.

This narrative is as much a personal family reflection as it is a professional reflection. I cited family stories throughout the text because over the course of many years my wife and kids routinely have provided moments of great insight and just as often great amusement. I am blessed to have such a wonderful, lively, active, and occasionally crazy family. As I was writing, I often made them stop whatever they were doing so they could listen to a paragraph or two and let me know how it sounded. That worked. Sometimes. Andrew, Nick, Ben, and Kate, never let go of imagination and curiosity and never ever forget that all of us are shaped by those we love and those who love us. Ann, your patience, wisdom, love, and extraordinary selflessness have always been the grounding of our home and family. With all my love, this book is for you!

Chapter 1 · A Liminal Moment

Epigraph. Charles Dickens, *A Tale of Two Cities* (New York: Signet Classic, 1960), p. 13.

1. Nassim Nicholas Taleb, *The Black Swan* (New York: Random House, 2007). Taleb's book provides a wonderful and colorful assessment of how people and organizations understand and approach risk and the unknown.

2. National Center for Education Statistics, *Digest of Education Statistics: 2013*, US Department of Education, Table 326.10, http://nces.ed.gov/programs/digest/d13 /tables/dt13_326.10.asp.

Chapter 2 · A Brief History of [Contemporary] Time

Epigraph. Lewis Carroll, *Alice's Adventures in Wonderland* (Bookbyte Digital Edition).

1. US Census Bureau, *Current Population Survey*, Table 2, www.census.gov /hhes/school/data/cps/1946/tab02-03.pdf.

2. US Census Bureau, *Current Population Survey*, Table 1, www.census.gov /hhes/school/data/cps/2011/tables.html.

3. National Center for Education Statistics, *Digest of Education Statistics: 2012*, US Department of Education, Table 306, http://nces.ed.gov/programs/digest/d12 /tables/dt12_306.asp.

4. National Center for Education Statistics, *Digest of Education Statistics: 2012*, US Department of Education, Table 223, http://nces.ed.gov/programs/digest /d12/tables/dt12_223.asp.

5. US Census Bureau, *Current Population Survey*, Table A-2, www.census.gov /hhes/socdemo/education/data/cps/historical/index.html.

6. US Census Bureau, *Current Population Survey*, Table A-6, www.census.gov /hhes/school/data/cps/historical/index.html. Data on annual population totals by age can be found at www.census.gov/popest/data/national/asrh/pre-1980/PE-11 .html.

7. National Center for Education Statistics, *Digest of Education Statistics: 2011*, US Department of Education, Table 209, http://nces.ed.gov/programs/digest/d11 /tables/dt11_209.asp.

8. The most notable public policy change of the period was the enactment of the Higher Education Act (HEA). Signed into law in November 1965 as part of President Lyndon Johnson's Great Society legislative push, the law sought "to strengthen the education resources of our colleges and universities and to provide financial assistance" (Public L. No. 89-239). Notably, the Higher Education Act created the framework for the Title IV federal financial aid programs that today assist millions of college students. For more information on the early history of the HEA, see www.pellinstitute.org/downloads/trio_clearinghouse-The%20 Early%20History%20of%20the%20Higher%20Education%20Act%20of%201965 .pdf.

9. US Census Bureau, *Current Population Survey*, Table A-2, www.census.gov /hhes/socdemo/education/data/cps/historical/index.html.

10. National Center for Education Statistics, *Digest of Education Statistics: 2011*, US Department of Education, Table 279, http://nces.ed.gov/programs/digest/d12 /tables/dt12_279.asp.

11. J. H. Pryor, S. Hurtado, V. B. Saenz, J. L. Santos, and W. S. Korn, *The American Freshman: Forty Year Trends* (Los Angeles: Higher Education Research Institute, UCLA, 2007).

12. *The College Advantage: Weathering the Economic Storm*, Georgetown University, Georgetown Public Policy Institute, Center on Education and the Workforce, August 2012, www9.georgetown.edu/grad/gppi/hpi/cew/pdfs /CollegeAdvantage.FullReport.081512.pdf.

13. *The College Payoff: Education, Occupations, Lifetime Earnings*, Georgetown University, Georgetown Public Policy Institute, Center on Education and the Workforce, August 2011, https://cew.georgetown.edu/report/the-college-payoff/.

14. "College Graduation: Weighing the Cost . . . and the Payoff," Pew Research Center, May 17, 2012, www.pewresearch.org/2012/05/17/college-graduation -weighing-the-cost-and-the-payoff/.

15. National Center for Education Statistics, *Digest of Education Statistics: 2011*, US Department of Education, Table 209, http://nces.ed.gov/programs/digest/d12 /tables/dt12_209.asp.

16. US Census Bureau, *Current Population Survey*, Table A-2, www.census.gov /hhes/socdemo/education/data/cps/historical/index.html.

17. James L. Heft, "Distinctively Catholic: Keeping the Faith in Higher Education," *Commonweal*, March 22, 2010, http://commonwealmagazine.org/distinctively -catholic.

18. Arthur Quiller-Couch, ed., 1919, *The Oxford Book of English Verse: 1250–1900*, www.bartleby.com/101/625.html.

19. National Center for Education Statistics, *Digest of Education Statistics: 2011*, US Department of Education, http://nces.ed.gov/programs/digest/2011menu _tables.asp. Postsecondary enrollment of students over age 24 (in both undergrad-

uate and graduate programs) rose by 31% between 1980 and 1990, compared to a gain of less than 4% in traditional-age enrollment. By 1990, older students made up 44% of all college students in the United States, compared to 38% a decade earlier (Table 200). Among the traditional-age population, though the number of high school graduates fell, those that did graduate went to college at rising rates. In 1977, half of all high school graduates enrolled in college somewhere within a year of finishing high school. By 1993, that number had reached nearly 63% (Table 209). Nearly all of the gains in enrollment over the period occurred among women. The number of female students enrolled in college rose by nearly 43% between 1977 and 1993, four times faster than the rate of increase among men over the same time period. The total number of male college students rose by just 11% over the same period (Table 198). In 1977, women made up 49% of all college students nationally. By 1993, they comprised 55% of all college students, a proportion that has continued to rise since then. Not only do more women enroll in college today than men, women enroll in college at much higher rates than men.

20. National Center for Education Statistics, *Digest of Education Statistics*, US Department of Education, Table 201 (Fall 2009), http://nces.ed.gov/programs/digest/d11/tables/dt11_201.asp, and Table 174 (Fall 1994), http://nces.ed.gov/programs/digest/d96/d96t174.asp.

21. Yahoo! Finance, custom tabulation, http://finance.yahoo.com/q/hp?s=%5EDJI+Historical+Prices.

22. Yahoo! Finance, custom tabulation, http://finance.yahoo.com/q/hp?s=%5EGSPC+Historical+Prices.

23. Yahoo! Finance, custom tabulation, http://finance.yahoo.com/q/hp?s=%5EIXIC+Historical+Prices.

24. *Economic Report of the President 2012*, Council of Economic Advisers, Table B-1, www.gpo.gov/fdsys/pkg/ERP-2012/content-detail.html.

25. *Economic Report of the President 2012*, Council of Economic Advisers, Table B-60, www.gpo.gov/fdsys/pkg/ERP-2012/content-detail.html.

26. *Economic Report of the President 2012*, Council of Economic Advisers, Table B-42, www.gpo.gov/fdsys/pkg/ERP-2012/content-detail.html.

27. Bureau of Labor Statistics, Labor Force Statistics from the *Current Population Survey*, custom tabulation from Federal Reserve Economic Data, St. Louis Federal Reserve Bank of St. Louis, http://research.stlouisfed.org/fred2/series/LNS14027662.

28. The National Bureau of Economic Research (NBER) has the enviable (or unenviable) task of dating business cycles. Among other things, their research identifies the beginning and ending dates of recessions and economic expansion. See www.nber.org/cycles/cyclesmain.html for a list of US business cycle expansions and contractions since 1857.

29. *State Higher Education Appropriations for 1992–93* and *State Higher Education Tax Appropriation Data for Fiscal Year 2008*, Grapevine, Center for the Study of Education Policy, Illinois State University, http://grapevine.illinoisstate.edu/tables/index.htm.

30. *State Expenditure Reports* (1993 and 2008), National Association of State Budget Officers, www.nasbo.org/publications-data/state-expenditure-report /archives.

31. US Census Bureau, "Income, Poverty, and Health Insurance in the United States: 2011," *Current Population Survey*, Tables F-9 and F-11, www.census.gov /hhes/www/income/data/historical/families/.

32. *Survey of Consumer Finances*, Federal Reserve Board, Data Tables 1 and 4, www.federalreserve.gov/econresdata/scf/scf_1992.htm.

33. S&P/Case-Shiller Home Price Indices, Seasonally Adjusted US National Index Levels, Q3 2012. The Case-Shiller Home Price Index tracks changes in the value of residential real estate nationally, www.standardandpoors.com/indices/sp -case-shiller-home-price-indices/en/us/?indexId=spusa-cashpidff—p-us—.

34. *Survey of Consumer Finances*, Federal Reserve Board, Data Table 7, www .federalreserve.gov/econresdata/scf/scf_1992.htm.

35. *Economic Report of the President 2012*, Council of Economic Advisers, Table B-77, www.gpo.gov/fdsys/pkg/ERP-2012/content-detail.html.

36. *Economic Report of the President 2012*, Council of Economic Advisers, Table B-2, www.gpo.gov/fdsys/pkg/ERP-2012/content-detail.html.

Chapter 3 · Demographic Disruption

Epigraph. Richard Rodriguez, *Darling: A Spiritual Autobiography* (New York: Viking Penguin, 2013), p. 26.

1. All of the data on projections of high school graduates and the changing racial and ethnic characteristics of high school graduates comes from the Western Interstate Commission for Higher Education. Brian T. Prescott and Peace Bransberger, *Knocking at the College Door: Projections of High School Graduates*, 8th ed. (Boulder, CO: Western Interstate Commission for Higher Education), 2012, www.wiche.edu/info/publications/knocking-8th/knocking-8th.pdf.

2. J. A. Martin, B. E. Hamilton, S. J. Ventura, et al., *Births: Final Data for 2010*, National Vital Statistics Reports, vol. 61, no. 1 (Hyattsville, MD: National Center for Health Statistics), August 28, 2012, www.cdc.gov/nchs/data/nvsr/nvsr61/nvsr61 _01.pdf.

3. Clearly immigration plays a role, as well. The Western Interstate Commission for Higher Education noted in its *Knocking on the College Door* report that Census Bureau data indicated that immigration accounted for 35% of the population growth in the United States between 2000 and 2009. Immigration particularly influenced the number of Hispanic high school graduates in the United States.

4. Improvements in high school retention rates, particularly among lower-income students, for example, could significantly influence the number of high school graduates, as could immigration.

5. J. H. Pryor, K. Eagan, L. Palucki Blake, S. Hurtado, J. Berdan, and M. H. Case, *The American Freshman: National Norms Fall 2012* (Los Angeles: Higher Education Research Institute, UCLA, 2012).

6. The expansion of online learning may change that equation, but for now and for the majority of new students, the college choice is limited to one institution at a time.

7. Approximately one-third of all students enrolled in four-year colleges and universities transfer institutions at least once before they receive a degree. Jennifer Gonzalez, "A Third of Students Transfer before Graduating, and Many Head toward Community Colleges," *The Chronicle of Higher Education*, February 28, 2012, http://chronicle.com/article/A-Third-of-Students-Transfer/130954/.

8. National Center for Education Statistics, *Digest of Education Statistics: 2012*, US Department of Education, Table 306, http://nces.ed.gov/programs/digest/d12/tables/dt12_306.asp.

9. Ping Ren, "Lifetime Mobility in the United States: 2010," *American Community Survey Briefs*, November 2011, Table 1, www.census.gov/prod/2011pubs/acsbr10-07.pdf.

10. All historic data on population by decade and state and region is collected by the Population Division of the US Census Bureau and are available at www.census.gov/popest/data/historical/index.html.

11. US Census Bureau, Population Division, Table 1, *Annual Estimates of the Population for the United States, Regions, States, and Puerto Rico: April 1, 2010 to July 1, 2012*, December 2012, www.census.gov/popest/index.html.

12. National Center for Education Statistics, *Digest of Education Statistics: 2011*, US Department of Education, Table 112, http://nces.ed.gov/programs/digest/d11/tables/dt11_112.asp. Note that these data are for public school graduates only. Graduates of nonpublic schools have, over the course of the last twenty years, comprised less than 10% of all high school graduates nationally.

13. *Knocking at the College Door*, appendix data tables, pages 72 to 75.

14. All data on high school graduate projections have been taken from *Knocking at the College Door*.

15. All data on distance from home to college have been taken from *The American Freshman: National Norms*.

16. The Higher Education Research Institute, which prepares *The American Freshman*, defines selectivity for four-year colleges and universities based on median SAT Verbal and Math scores or ACT scores. Their stratification defines approximately 36% of all colleges and universities as having low or very low selectivity. Thirty-nine percent of all institutions were identified as either highly or very highly selective. For additional information, see Appendix A of *The American Freshman: National Norms Fall 2013*, www.heri.ucla.edu/monographs/TheAmericanFreshman2013.pdf.

17. A much higher proportion of high school graduates enroll in college today than did in 1970. These data suggest that, as the number of college students has increased, most have chosen to enroll in institutions located close to home. And, as enrollment has increased, many institutions, particularly public institutions, have grown substantially in size to accommodate the growing demand.

18. Pryor, Eagan, Palucki Blake, Hurtado, Berdan, and Case, *The American Freshman.*

19. National Center for Education Statistics, *Digest of Education Statistics: 2013*, US Department of Education, Table 306.10, http://nces.ed.gov/programs/digest/d13/tables/dt13_306.10.asp. For purposes of federal reporting, international students are described by the decidedly inelegant term "non-resident alien."

20. Institute of International Education, "Top 25 Places of Origin of International Students, 2012/13–2013/14," *Open Doors Report on International Educational Exchange*, 2014, www.iie.org/Research-and-Publications/Open-Doors/Data/International-Students/Leading-Places-of-Origin/2012-14.

21. For an overview of the steps international students and institutions must follow, visit the US Immigration and Customs Enforcement (ICE) website at www.ice.gov/sevis/students/.

22. US Central Intelligence Agency, *The World Factbook*, www.cia.gov/library/publications/the-world-factbook/geos/ch.html.

23. *New York Times*, "President Exit Polls," http://elections.nytimes.com/2012/results/president/exit-polls, accessed February 5, 2013.

24. A term used by the Census Bureau that is inclusive of race and ethnicity. It includes all people who are nonwhite alone, Hispanic, or of multiple race or ethnicity. The inverse would be white alone and non-Hispanic.

25. Karen R. Humes, Nicholas P. Jones, and Robert R. Ramirez, *Overview of Race and Hispanic Origin: 2010*, 2010 Census Briefs, US Census Bureau, March 2011, www.census.gov/prod/cen2010/briefs/c2010br-02.pdf.

26. US Census Bureau press release, "Most Children Younger than Age 1 are Minorities, Census Bureau Reports," May 17, 2012, www.census.gov/newsroom/releases/archives/population/cb12-90.html.

27. US Census Bureau, *Age and Sex Composition in the United States: 2011*, www.census.gov/population/age/data/2011comp.html.

28. All data on projections of high school graduates by race and ethnicity have been derived from tables prepared by WICHE in their *Knocking on the College Door* report (2012). The data reflect public school graduates only.

29. Rates of high school completion differ, sometimes significantly, by race and ethnicity and family income. WICHE projections of high school graduates assume that current rates of school progress and completion will continue. Clearly, changes in high school drop-out rates, up or down, could significantly change the number of high school graduates.

30. Minnesota Department of Education, Data Center, District Level Tabulation, prepared February 13, 2013, http://w20.education.state.mn.us/MDEAnalytics/Data.jsp.

31. The US Census Bureau reports on a variety of similar, though not always identical, population totals by race and ethnicity. The numbers vary by the time period in which they were collected and in relation to whether they were collected by single race alone or by race in combination with another race. These data were collected in the 2011 *Current Population Survey* and accessed on February 13, 2013,

at www.census.gov/population/race/. They reflect singular race and ethnicity, not in combination with other races.

32. Jeffrey S. Passel, D'Vera Cohn, and Mark Hugo Lopez, Pew Hispanic Center, "Census 2010: 50 Million Latinos Hispanics Account for More Than Half of Nation's Growth in Past Decade," March 24, 2011, www.pewhispanic.org/2011/03 /24/hispanics-account-for-more-than-half-of-nations-growth-in-past-decade/.

33. US Census Bureau press release, "2010 Census Shows America's Diversity," March 24, 2011, www.census.gov/newsroom/releases/archives/2010_census/cb11 -cn125.html.

34. Pew Research Hispanic Center, Data Gallery, accessed on February 13, 2013, at www.pewhispanic.org/.

35. US Census Bureau, *Age and Sex Composition in the United States: 2011*, www.census.gov/population/age/data/2011comp.html.

36. B. E. Hamilton, J. A. Martin, and S. J. Ventura, *Births: Preliminary Data for 2011*, National Vital Statistics Reports, vol. 61, no. 5 (Hyattsville, MD: National Center for Health Statistics), October 3, 2012, www.cdc.gov/nchs/data/nvsr/nvsr61 /nvsr61_05.pdf.

37. National Center for Education Statistics, *Digest of Education Statistics: 2011*, US Department of Education, Table 44, http://nces.ed.gov/programs/digest/d11 /tables/dt11_044.asp.

38. Mark Hugo Lopez, Pew Research Hispanic Center, "Latinos and Education: Explaining the Attainment Gap," October 7, 2009, www.pewhispanic.org/2009/10 /07/latinos-and-education-explaining-the-attainment-gap/.

39. National Center for Education Statistics, *Digest of Educational Statistics: 2013*, US Department of Education, Table 306.10, http://nces.ed.gov/programs /digest/d13/tables/dt13_306.10.asp.

40. Lopez, "Latinos and Education."

41. National Center for Education Statistics, *Digest of Educational Statistics: 2013*, US Department of Education, Table 306.50, http://nces.ed.gov/programs /digest/d13/tables/dt13_306.50.asp.

42. National Center for Education Statistics, *Digest of Educational Statistics: 2012*, US Department of Education, Table 376, http://nces.ed.gov/programs/digest /d12/tables/dt12_376.asp.

43. US Census Bureau, *Current Population Survey*, 2012 Annual Social and Economic Supplement, Table 1, "Educational Attainment of the Population 18 Years and Over, by Age, Sex, Race and Hispanic Origin: 2012," www.census.gov /hhes/socdemo/education/data/cps/2012/tables.html.

44. US Census Bureau, *Current Population Survey*, 2012 Annual Social and Economic Supplement, Table FINC-03, "Presence of Related Children Under 18 Years Old—All Families by Total Money Income in 2012, Type of Family, Work Experience in 2012, Race and Hispanic Origin of Reference Person," www.census .gov/hhes/www/cpstables/032013/faminc/finc03_000.htm.

45. Postsecondary Education Opportunity, no. 245, "Family Income and Unequal Educational Opportunity, 1970 to 2011," November 2012, www.postsecondary.org

/last12/245_1112pg1_20.pdf. College participation rates are derived from the product of high school completion rates and college continuation rates. They provide a much broader measure of college access than continuation rates alone because they take into account progression within high school among all students (which varies by income) as well as progression to college among those who complete high school.

46. US Census Bureau, *Current Population Survey*, 2012 Annual Social and Economic Supplement, Table FINC-03, "Presence of Related Children Under 18 Years Old—All Families by Total Money Income in 2012, Type of Family, Work Experience in 2012, Race and Hispanic Origin of Reference Person," www.census .gov/hhes/www/cpstables/032013/faminc/finc03_000.htm.

Chapter 4 · Economic Disruption

Epigraph. Will Rogers Memorial Museums website. Accessed on February 15, 2013 at www.willrogers.com/says/will_says.html.

1. Lumina Foundation and Gallup, "America's Call for Higher Education Redesign," February 5, 2013, www.luminafoundation.org/publications/Americas _Call_for_Higher_Education_Redesign.pdf.

2. Pew Research Center, "Is College Worth It?," May 16, 2011, www.pewsocial trends.org/files/2011/05/higher-ed-report.pdf.

3. Sallie Mae and Ipsos Public Affairs, *How America Pays for College 2012*, July 2012, Table 22, www1.salliemae.com/about/news_info/research/how_America_pays/.

4. Pew Research Center, "Is College Worth It?"

5. Sallie Mae and Ipsos Public Affairs, *How America Pays for College 2012*.

6. Sallie Mae and Ipsos Public Affairs, *How America Pays for College 2012*. Parents, perhaps fearful of their children moving home to live with them, were the most skeptical of the intellectual and social value of college. Only 19% strongly agreed that they would send their children to college for the intellectual and social experience regardless of the whether they earned more money with the degree. Fully 30% of all students and parents disagreed with the question altogether, indicating that were it not for the hope or opportunity for economic return, they would not go to college.

7. J. H. Pryor, K. Eagan, L. Palucki Blake, S. Hurtado, J. Berdan, and M. H. Case, *The American Freshman: National Norms Fall 2012* (Los Angeles: Higher Education Research Institute, UCLA, 2012).

8. US Census Bureau, *Current Population Survey*, Annual Social and Economic Supplements, Table F-7, www.census.gov/hhes/www/income/data /historical/families/.

9. US Census Bureau, *Current Population Survey*, Annual Social and Economic Supplements, Table F-9, www.census.gov/hhes/www/income/data/historical /families/.

10. Author's tabulations. Income data from US Census Bureau, *Current Population Survey*, Annual Social and Economic Supplements, Table F-3, www.census.gov/hhes/www/income/data/historical/families/. Cost of attendance

data from National Center for Education Statistics, *Digest of Education Statistics: 2013*, US Department of Education, Table 330.10, http://nces.ed.gov/programs/digest /d13/tables/dt13_330.10.asp. For public colleges and universities, the data reflect in-state tuition and fees. The data for private colleges include only not-for-profit institutions.

11. Jesse Bricker, Arthur B. Kennickell, Kevin B. Moore, and John Sabelhaus, "Changes in U.S. Family Finances from 2007 to 2010: Evidence from the Survey of Consumer Finances," *Federal Reserve Bulletin*, vol. 98, no. 2, June 2012, Table 7, www.federalreserve.gov/pubs/bulletin/2012/pdf/scf12.pdf.

12. Bricker, Kennickell, Moore, and Sabelhaus, "Changes in U.S. Family Finances from 2007 to 2010," Tables 9 and 9.1.

13. S&P/Case-Shiller Home Price Indices, US National Index Levels, www .standardandpoors.com/indices/sp-case-shiller-home-price-indices/en/us/ ?indexId=spusa-cashpidff—p-us—-.

14. S&P/Case-Shiller Home Price Indices, Seasonally Adjusted US National Index Levels, Q3 2012, www.standardandpoors.com/indices/sp-case-shiller-home -price-indices/en/us/?indexId=spusa-cashpidff—p-us—-.

15. Bricker, Kennickell, Moore, and Sabelhaus, "Changes in U.S. Family Finances from 2007 to 2010," p. 59.

16. "Underwater Mortgage Rates Declined in 2nd-Quarter," *Bloomberg Business-week*, September 12, 2012, www.businessweek.com/ap/2012-09-12/underwater -mortgages-declined-in-2nd-quarter.

17. Bricker, Kennickell, Moore, and Sabelhaus, "Changes in U.S. Family Finances from 2007 to 2010," Table 4.

18. "Savings at Lowest Rate since Depression," *CBS News*, February 1, 2007, www.cbsnews.com/stories/2007/02/01/business/main2422489.shtml. I share this story with the gracious approval of my brother and sister-in-law.

19. US Department of Commerce, Bureau of Economic Analysis, data compiled by the Economic Research Division of the Federal Reserve Bank of St. Louis and available on its Federal Reserve Economic Data (FRED) website at http:// research.stlouisfed.org/fred2/series/PSAVERT.

20. Bricker, Kennickell, Moore, and Sabelhaus, "Changes in U.S. Family Finances from 2007 to 2010," p. 15.

21. According to the *Survey of Consumer Finances*, half of all American families reported in 2010 that they had retirement accounts. Nearly 20% also said they held cash value insurance policies. However, neither of those typically would be available to support college expenses.

22. Employee Benefit Research Institute and Mathew Greenwald & Associates, Inc., 2012 Retirement Confidence Survey, *Issue Brief*, no. 369, March 2012, www.ebri.org/surveys/rcs/.

23. US Department of Labor, Bureau of Labor Statistics, data compiled by the Economic Research Division of the Federal Reserve Bank of St. Louis and available on their Federal Reserve Economic Data (FRED) website at http:// research.stlouisfed.org/fred2/search?st=unemployment.

24. US Department of Labor, Bureau of Labor Statistics, *The Employment Situation—January 2013*, February 1, 2013.

25. National Employment Law Project, Data Brief, "The Low-Wage Recovery and Growing Inequality," August 2012, www.nelp.org/page/-/Job_Creation /LowWageRecovery2012.pdf?nocdn=1.

26. Donghoon Lee, "Household Debt and Credit: Student Debt," Federal Reserve Bank of New York, February 28, 2013, www.newyorkfed.org/newsevents /mediaadvisory/2013/Lee022813.pdf.

27. The Institute for College Access & Success, The Project on Student Debt, "Student Debt and the Class of 2011," October 2012, http://projectonstudentdebt.org/.

28. The College Board Advocacy and Policy Center, *Trends in Student Aid, 2012*, October 2012, http://trends.collegeboard.org/sites/default/files/student-aid -2012-full-report-130201.pdf.

29. The College Board Advocacy and Policy Center, *Trends in Student Aid, 2012*, October 2012.

30. The College Board Advocacy and Policy Center, *Trends in Student Aid, 2012*, October 2012.

31. *Economic Report of the President 2013*, Council of Economic Advisers, Table B-77, www.whitehouse.gov/sites/default/files/docs/erp2013/full_2013_economic _report_of_the_president.pdf.

32. Joint Economic Committee Democratic Staff, United States Congress, "The Causes and Consequences of Increasing Student Debt," June 2013, www.jec.senate .gov/public//index.cfm?a=Files.Serve&File_id=02b28db4-b32b-4dca-b595 -a390b6f4ca98.

33. The College Board Advocacy and Policy Center, *Trends in College Pricing, 2014*, October 2014, https://secure-media.collegeboard.org/digitalServices/misc /trends/2014-trends-college-pricing-report-final.pdf.

Chapter 5 · Cultural Disruption

Epigraph. Philipp Frank, *Einstein: His Life and Times* (New York: Alfred A. Knopf, 1947), p. 185. Einstein was responding to Thomas Edison's assertion that a college education is useless.

1. Merriam-Webster online, www.merriam-webster.com/dictionary/commodity.

2. Data from Peterson's online college search. Accessed on March 5, 2013, and available at www.petersons.com/college-search.aspx.

3. W. Chan Kim and Renee Mauborgne, "Blue Ocean Strategy," *Harvard Business Review*, October 2004.

4. Youngme Moon, *Different: Escaping the Competitive Herd* (New York: Crown Publishing Group, 2010).

5. Sallie Mae and Ipsos Public Affairs, *How America Pays for College 2012*, July 2012, www1.salliemae.com/about/news_info/research/how_America_pays/. In total, 87% of parents and students strongly agreed or somewhat agreed that a

college degree was necessary for a desired occupation. Ninety-two percent strongly agreed or somewhat agreed that they were attending college because they would earn more money with a college degree.

6. J. Immerwahr and J. Johnson, "Squeeze Play 2010: Continued Public Anxiety on Cost, Harsher Judgments on How Colleges Are Run," Joint Project of the National Center for Public Policy and Higher Education and Public Agenda, February 2010, www.publicagenda.org/files/SqueezePlay2010report.pdf.

7. Pew Research Center, "Is College Worth It?," May 16, 2011, www.pewsocial trends.org/files/2011/05/higher-ed-report.pdf.

8. K. Eagan, E. B. Stolzenberg, J. J. Ramirez, M. C. Aragon, R. S. Suchard, and S. Hurtado, *The American Freshman: National Norms Fall 2014*, Los Angeles: Higher Education Research Institute, UCLA, February 2015.

9. *The College Advantage: Weathering the Economic Storm*, Georgetown University, Georgetown Public Policy Institute, Center on Education and the Workforce, August 2012, www9.georgetown.edu/grad/gppi/hpi/cew/pdfs /CollegeAdvantage.FullReport.081512.pdf.

10. US Department of Labor, Bureau of Labor Statistics, *The Employment Situation—February 2013*, March 8, 2013, www.bls.gov/bls/newsrels.htm#OEUS.

11. US Department of Labor, Bureau of Labor Statistics, data compiled by the Economic Research Division of the Federal Reserve Bank of St. Louis and available on their Federal Reserve Economic Data (FRED) website at http://research.stlouisfed .org/fred2/search?st=unemployment.

12. Pew Research Center, "Is College Worth It?"

13. Thomas Edison quoted in the July 9, 1913, issue of the *New York Dramatic Mirror*. He had been asked to speculate on the future as part of a series of articles about the (then new) motion picture. See Quote Investigator at http://quote investigator.com/2012/02/15/books-obsolete/ for a more detailed description of Edison's prognostication and subsequent references to it.

14. I. E. Allen and J. Seaman, Babson Survey Research Group, *Changing Course: Ten Years of Tracking Online Education in the United States*, January 2013, www.onlinelearningsurvey.com/reports/changingcourse.pdf.

15. *US News and World Report*, "Best Online Bachelor's Programs," 2013, www .usnews.com/education/online-education/bachelors/rankings?int=a29209.

16. G. Blumenstyk, "Starbucks Will Send Thousands of Employees to Arizona State for Degrees," *The Chronicle of Higher Education*, June 15, 2014, http:// chronicle.com/article/Starbucks-Will-Send-Thousands/147151/?cid=at&utm _source=at&utm_medium=en.

17. Clayton M. Christensen and Henry J. Eyring, *The Innovative University: Changing the DNA of Higher Education from the Inside Out* (San Francisco: Jossey-Bass, 2011).

18. Joseph A. Schumpeter, *Capitalism, Socialism, and Democracy* (New York: Harper & Brothers, 1947). Creative destruction describes economic innovation and business cycles—a process of continuous invention, destruction, and renewal.

19. Caroline Hoxby, "The Economics of Online Postsecondary Education: MOOCs, Nonselective Education, and Highly Selective Education," January 2014, National Bureau of Economic Research Working Paper No. 19816, www.nber.org /papers/w19816.

Chapter 6 · No Line on the Horizon

Epigraph. Stephen B. Crane, "I Saw a Man Pursuing the Horizon," accessed at www.poetryfoundation.org.

1. J. R. Abel and R. Deitz, "Do the Benefits of College Still Outweigh the Costs?," Federal Reserve Bank of New York, *Current Issues in Economics and Finance*, vol. 20, no. 3, 2014, www.newyorkfed.org/research/current_issues.

2. D. Carroll and A. Higgins, "A College Education Saddles Young Households with Debt, but Still Pays Off," Federal Reserve Bank of Cleveland, Economic Trends, July 16, 2014, www.clevelandfed.org/research/trends/2014/0714/011abmar.cfm.

3. *The College Payoff: Education, Occupations, Lifetime Earnings*, Georgetown University, Georgetown Public Policy Institute, Center on Education and the Workforce, August 2011, https://cew.georgetown.edu/report/the-college-payoff/.

4. J. H. Pryor, K. Eagan, L. Palucki Blake, S. Hurtado, J. Berdan, and M .H. Case, *The American Freshman: National Norms Fall 2012* (Los Angeles: Higher Education Research Institute, UCLA, 2012).

5. For a wonderful summary of the difficulty of making a decision when faced with many choices, read Barry Schwartz, *The Paradox of Choice: Why More Is Less* (HarperCollins: New York, 2004).

6. J. H. Pryor, S. Hurtado, V. B. Saenz, J. L. Santos, and W. S. Korn, *The American Freshman: Forty Year Trends* (Los Angeles: Higher Education Research Institute, UCLA, 2007).

7. These figures are derived from unpublished data collected by the Minnesota Private College Council. However, they also are available from the federal IPEDS *Institutional Characteristics* survey, http://nces.ed.gov/ipeds/datacenter/.

8. In simple terms, price elasticity of demand measures the change in demand for a good or service with a unit change in price. Demand that changes little as price changes is commonly described as inelastic. Demand that changes more significantly as price changes is described as elastic. Financial aid mediates the elasticity of demand at colleges and universities, though data indicating wide-spread institutional deselection prior to the receipt of financial aid indicates the influence of sticker price on choice and elasticity.

9. This figure comes after making modest assumptions about family assets.

10. National Center for Education Statistics, *The Condition of Education: 2012*, US Department of Education, Indicator 41, http://nces.ed.gov/pubs2012/2012045_4 .pdf.

11. The College Board, Advocacy and Policy Center, *Trends in Student Aid, 2012*, October 2012, Table 1A, http://trends.collegeboard.org/sites/default/files /student-aid-2012-full-report.pdf.

12. Pryor, Eagan, Palucki Blake, Hurtado, Berdan, and Case, *The American Freshman: National Norms Fall 2012.*

13. Sallie Mae and Ipsos Public Affairs, *How America Pays for College 2012*, July 2012, Table 20, www1.salliemae.com/about/news_info/research/how_America _pays/.

14. Tuition cuts typically receive the most attention because they represent the most dramatic approach to pricing change. For a description of recent price cuts and how they have been implemented at different campuses, see the *Wall Street Journal*, "Colleges Try Cutting Tuition—and Aid Packages," October 11, 2013, www.wsj.com/articles/SB10001424052702303643304579107683540651404.

15. Pew Research Center, "Is College Worth It?," May 16, 2011, Question 8: "Compared with 10 years ago, would you say the value students get for the money they spend on a college education today is . . . ?" Results were quite consistent across institutional type, though presidents of two-year institutions were least likely to describe the value of college today as better than a decade ago. Report available at www.pewsocialtrends.org/files/2011/05/higher-ed-report.pdf.

Chapter 7 · Toward a New Marketplace

Epigraph. Jim Collins, *How the Mighty Fall* (New York: HarperCollins, 2009), pp. 119–20.

1. Many thanks to my friend, Brian Zucker, principal of Human Capital, Inc., for helping to conceive and develop this chart, which we first presented together at the Midwest Regional Forum of the College Board in February 2012.

Chapter 8 · Reimagine the Future

Epigraphs. Walter Isaacson, *Steve Jobs* (New York: Simon & Schuster, 2011), p. 329; Friedrich Nietzsche, *Daybreak: Thoughts on the Prejudices of Morality*, translated by R. J. Hollingdale (New York: Cambridge University Press, 1982), p. 153.

1. Clayton M. Christensen and Henry J. Eyring, *The Innovative University: Changing the DNA of Higher Education from the Inside Out* (San Francisco: Jossey-Bass, 2011). Christensen and Eyring make a particularly compelling and insightful case for using the DNA metaphor to describe the development and operation of the contemporary higher education model.

2. Christensen and Eyring, *The Innovative University.*

3. Youngme Moon, *Different: Escaping the Competitive Herd* (New York: Crown Publishing Group, 2010).

4. Isaacson, *Steve Jobs.*

5. Between September 1997, when Steve Jobs returned as CEO of Apple, and his resignation shortly before his death in October 2011, Apple stock shares gained nearly 6700% ("What if you had bought Apple stock in 1997?" MSN Money online, http://money.msn.com/top-stocks/post.aspx?post=7ba70f76-54af-4065-baad -922b90a789b5).

6. W. Chan Kim and Renee Mauborgne, "Blue Ocean Strategy," *Harvard Business Review*, October 2004. Followed by a book of the same name, Kim and Mauborgne describe the imperative for creating "blue ocean," or uncontested, market space. They provide numerous examples of companies that succeeded in breaking out of the commodity trap—which turns similar products into commodities and reduces competition to pricing. Most importantly, they emphasize the role of strategy, not tactics, in creating blue ocean spaces.

7. National Geographic online, "Genes Are Us. And Them," http://ngm .nationalgeographic.com/2013/07/125-explore/shared-genes. The story is fascinating and squirm inducing.

8. Each of these statements appear on actual college websites.

9. Next best choice is particularly important. Too much market research focuses only on the absolute importance or value of college characteristics rather than their comparative importance. For example, many first-year college students will identify "academic reputation" as important to their college choice. But what is most important to an institution is how a prospective student evaluates its academic reputation in comparison to another, next best choice institution. Am I better or worse or the same?

10. Kevin Menk, principal of Strategic Resource Partners, provided invaluable insight for this model detailing the temporal elements of college choice.

11. The proprietary research was conducted by Strategic Resource Partners and Hardwick Day for Minnesota's private colleges in fall 2009. More than 200 Minnesota parents of middle school students were randomly selected and surveyed. The survey also included parents of high school students and was designed to assess family behaviors and attitudes regarding the selection and financing of higher education.

12. ACT, Inc., *The Condition of College & Career Readiness, 2012*, www.act.org /research-policy/college-career-readiness-report-2012/. The ACT organization defines college readiness as the knowledge and skills a student needs to enroll and succeed in credit-bearing first-year college courses without the need for remediation. Benchmarks represent the minimum score required on subject tests to indicate a 50% chance or better in obtaining a grade of B or higher in a credit-bearing first-year college course. Nearly 1.7 million high school graduates took the ACT in 2012.

13. The College Board, "SAT® Report: Only 43 Percent of 2012 College-Bound Seniors Are College Ready," September 24, 2012, http://press.collegeboard.org/releases /2012/sat-report-only-43-percent-2012-college-bound-seniors-college-ready.

14. ACT, Inc., *College and Career Readiness: The Importance of Early Learning*, Policy Report, February 2013, www.act.org/research-policy/policy-publications/.

15. National Center for Education Statistics, *Digest of Education Statistics: 2012*, US Department of Education, Table 375, http://nces.ed.gov/programs/digest/d12 /tables/dt12_375.asp.

16. Howard Bowen, *The Costs of Higher Education* (San Francisco: Jossey-Bass Publishers, 1980), p. 19.

17. National Association of College and University Business Officers, *2012 NACUBO-Commonfund Study of Endowments*, January 2013. Eight hundred five US institutions provided data for the study. The study's endowment findings were published in the *Chronicle of Higher Education* on February 1, 2013, http://chronicle.com/article/In-a-Volatile-Economy/136941/.

18. The College Board Advocacy and Policy Center, *Trends in Student Aid, 2013*, October 2013, p. 28, http://trends.collegeboard.org/sites/default/files/student-aid-2013-full-report.pdf.

19. National Center for Education Statistics, *The Condition of Education: 2012*, US Department of Education, Indicator 41, Table A-41-1, http://nces.ed.gov/pubs2012/2012045.pdf.

20. Robert B. Archibold and David H. Feldman, *Why Does College Cost So Much?* (New York: Oxford University Press, 2011).

21. Jon McGee, "Disruptive Adaptation: The New Market for Higher Education," *Lawlor Perspective*, The Lawlor Group, June 2012, www.thelawlorgroup.com/disruptive-adaptation-new-market-higher-education.

Chapter 9 · Breakpoint

Epigraphs. Dictionary.com, *Columbia World of Quotations* (Columbia University Press, 1996), http://quotes.dictionary.com/He_is_the_best_man_who_when_making; Youngme Moon, *Different: Escaping the Competitive Herd* (New York: Crown Publishing Group, 2010).

ability to pay, 7, 43, 44–45, 88–92. *See also* financial aid; prices, college and university

accessibility, in higher education, 3, 4, 48, 51, 63

accountability, in higher education, 4, 84–85, 95–99

ACT: College Readiness Benchmarks, 127; test scores, 122, 128, 153n16

admissions marketplace, 96, 117–21; applications process, 25–28, 85–87, 91, 124. *See also* enrollment; recruitment

affordability, of higher education, 3–4, 7, 43–45, 48, 51, 63, 132–35. *See also* ability to pay; prices, college and university

American Freshman, The (UCLA Higher Education Research Institute), 31

American Indian / Alaskan Native student population, 36

Apple Corporation, as example of differentiation, 111–13, 161n5

applications: for admission, 25–28, 85–87, 91, 124; for financial aid, 88–89, 123, 133

appropriations, government. *See* government, federal and state: appropriations from

aptitude, student, 65, 66–67

Asian student population, 35, 37, 39, 40–41

aspirations, college and university, aligning operations with, 2, 5, 12, 101, 136, 142

aspirations, student, 38, 39, 65, 66–67, 75, 122, 129

black student population, 37, 39, 40–41

borrowing. *See* debt

Bowen, Howard, Revenue Theory of Cost, 131–32

Carnegie Classification system, 114

Case-Shiller Home Price Index, 152n33

choices, student: factors involved in, 8, 56, 68, 117–18, 122; families' input, 5, 7, 26–29, 117–20; location's importance to, 28–32, 153n17; mitigating risk in, 125; price sensitivity affecting, 91–92, 94, 96, 160n8; rankings affecting, 70–71, 162n9; selectivity principle, 31, 87, 124, 153n16. *See also* applications; enrollment; recruitment

Christensen, Clayton, 78, 109

College Board: College Readiness Benchmarks, 127–28; financial aid data from, 61, 90–91

College of Saint Benedict (Minnesota), profile of students, 32, 124

colleges and universities: Great Recession of 2008's effects on, 17–18, 19, 20–21; increase in numbers of, 8, 9–10, 27; location of, 28–32, 153n17; rankings, 69–71, 78, 113, 131, 162n9; revenues, 3, 4, 63, 93–94, 110, 130–32, 135–36; values and attributes of, 3, 66–67, 76, 103. *See also* choices, student; context, collegiate; higher education; management, college and university; marketplace, college and university; mission, college and university; prices, college and university; private colleges and universities; public colleges and universities

commoditization, of higher education, 5, 9–10, 11–12, 64, 67–71, 162n6

comparative advantage, building, 115–21, 130. *See also* difference/differentiation, in higher education

Congressional Joint Economic Committee Democratic Staff, report on student debt, 60

Consumer Price Index, 14. *See also* inflation

context, collegiate, 92, 101, 102; changes in, 21, 65–67; management-related, 5, 19

costs, college and university. *See* prices, college and university

crisis, language of, 20–21

culture: American, 11–12, 35, 62, 65, 69, 70, 84; campus, 67, 69, 118, 124–25

debt: consumer, 16, 59–60; student, 48, 57–63, 91

decision making, by colleges and universities: budgetary, 130–32, 138–39; constraints on, 104, 108–11; economic trends and, 17–18; effective, 2, 140–41; framework for, 104–6; issues driving, 7, 12, 103–4; market-based, 5–6; recruitment process and, 117–21; risk involved in, 2, 19, 119. *See also* leadership, college and university; management, college and university

difference/differentiation, in higher education: achieving goal of, 124–25; advertising's creation of, 67–68; Apple as example of, 111–13, 161n5; creating, 67–71, 124–25; economic, 58, 60, 63, 79, 88, 131; importance of, 1–2, 5, 111–14; reimagining, 115–21, 130

disruption(s), 1–2, 20–21, 83–85, 88, 100–101; adaptations to, 101–4, 117, 121, 141, 143; cultural, 35, 64–82, 137–39; demographic, 12–13, 22–41, 63, 64, 94; economic, 42–63, 64, 91, 94, 132, 139; and future of higher education, 83–99; technological, 64, 67–68, 77–82

distinction. *See* difference/differentiation, in higher education

economy (US), 13–21, 159n18. *See also* disruption(s), economic; employment; Great Recession of 2008; stock market; unemployment; *and specific economic indicators*

education. *See* colleges and universities; higher education

effectiveness, in higher education, 2, 138, 139

efficiency, in higher education, 2, 64–65, 136, 138, 139

Employee Benefit Research Institute, survey of savings and investments, 55

employment, college education's enhancement of, 10, 14, 17, 71–73. *See also* unemployment

endowments, higher education, 17, 49, 132, 135–36

enrollment: factors affecting, 25–28; geographic trends in, 28–34; goals for, 22, 32, 34, 69, 85–88; increasing, 5, 8, 9–10, 12–13, 17, 71, 153n17; instability in, 84–85, 85–88; of lower-income students, 40–41, 44; preparation for, 126–30, 162nn11–12; price sensitivity as threat to, 92; profile of, 122–23; racial and ethnic diversity in, 34, 35–39; of traditional-age students, 15, 24, 41, 151n19; by women, 9, 10, 13, 151n19. *See also* admissions marketplace; recruitment

equilibrium, in higher education, 4–5, 130–32, 142–43

Eyring, Henry J., 109

families: changing expectations of, 95–99, 117; economic characteristics of, 39–40, 59; input on college choice, 5, 7, 26–29, 117–20; paying for college, 11, 43–56, 60–62, 63, 84–94, 132–35, 143; preparing children for college, 126–30, 162nn11–12; value concerns of, 72–76, 119–20. *See also* home prices/values; income, family; net worth, family

Federal Reserve Bank of New York, reports on college economics, 57, 58, 85

financial aid: applications for, 88–89, 123, 133; increasing demand for, 69, 88–94, 133, 134, 135; necessity of, 43, 44, 47; strategies for, 3–4. *See also* government, federal and state: appropriations from; taxpayers, support of higher education by

Freakonomics (Levitt and Dubner), 143

fund-raising. *See* endowments, higher education

Georgetown University Center on Education and the Workforce, report on college graduates' earnings, 10–11

government, federal and state: appropriations from, 17, 61, 63, 89, 91, 150n8; regulation of higher education, 4, 93–94, 96–99. *See also* taxpayers, support of higher education by

Great Recession of 2008: disruptions caused by, 62–63; family income affected by, 45, 46–48; finding new equilibrium after, 143; impacts on higher education, 2–3, 18–21, 43, 83; unemployment rates during, 10

Gross Domestic Product (GDP), 14, 16, 18

Heft, James L., on commercialization of American culture, 11–12 higher education: demand for, 25–28, 85–88; differential thinking in, 102–3, 107–41; economics of, 43, 131–32, 143; equilibrium in, 4–5, 130–32, 142–43; expectations of, 8–12, 71, 95–99; future trends in, 83–99; government regulation of, 4, 93–94, 96–99; issues facing, 3–5, 6–7; online, 64, 67–68, 77–82, 153n6; organizational genome of, 108–11, 113–15, 161n1; transactional narrative of, 71–76, 80, 82; transformational narrative of, 5, 10, 11, 75. *See also* colleges and universities; commoditization, of higher education; difference/ differentiation, in higher education; value, of higher education

Higher Education Act of 1965, 96–97, 150n8

Higher Education Opportunity Act of 2008, 97–98

high school-to-college participation rates, 9, 13, 24, 156n45

Hispanic student population, 36, 37–39, 40–41, 152n3

home prices/values, 16, 152n33; Great Recession's effects on, 18, 50–51, 61

Hoxby, Caroline, on MOOCs, 80

immigration, to US, 28, 32–34, 39, 152n3

income, family: college costs in relation to, 3, 40–41, 45, 46–48, 53, 62, 89, 90–91; flat or falling, 47, 48, 51, 61, 62–63, 132; increases in, 10–11, 13, 14, 15, 16, 48. *See also* net worth, family; savings, personal

inflation: family income compared to, 15–16, 46–47; personal savings rates compared to, 53, 55; pre-Great Recession levels, 14; price of college compared to, 3, 60, 61

Institute for College Access and Success (TICAS), report on student loan debt, 57

Internet, 10, 26, 79, 86. *See also* higher education: online

investment(s): in admissions marketing, 87, 105; college degree seen as, 43, 45, 47–48, 60–63, 72–74; family/personal, 25, 54–55, 132. *See also* endowments, higher education; net worth, family; return on investment (ROI), from college education; savings, personal; stock market

leadership, college and university: adaptations by, 101–4, 138, 140; concerns over student debt,

61–62, 63; threats to, 109–11. *See also* decision making, by colleges and universities; management, college and university

location, colleges and universities, importance of, 28–32, 153n17

management, college and university: aligning aspirations and operations, 2, 5, 12, 101, 136, 142; context for, 5, 19; expense-side, 136, 139; forces influencing, 7, 18, 83; government regulation of, 97, 98; practices of, 114; reimagining, 19, 130–32, 142–43; student expectations of, 100. *See also* decision making, by colleges and universities; leadership, college and university

marketing, by colleges and universities, 8, 12–13, 27. *See also* recruitment

marketplace, college and university: adaptations by, 102, 103, 104; challenges in, 24, 27–28, 136; changing, 2–3, 6, 23, 25, 36, 84–99, 101, 142–43; choices facing, 5–7, 28, 112; development of, 130–32; establishing distinction in, 119–22, 140; expectations of, 67, 75, 95, 126, 139, 142; forces shaping, 2–3, 18, 21, 22, 58, 83, 127; new, 4–5, 12, 111, 112, 136, 142; regional demographics affecting, 28–32; reimagining, 6, 100–107, 121–30, 141–42; values of, 66–67, 115. *See also* admissions marketplace; commoditization, of higher education

massively open online courses (MOOCs), 79–82

middle class: college seen as gateway to, 10, 40, 45, 56; savings habits of, 52

migration, within US, 28–30

Minnesota Private College Research Foundation, study of middle school students' college preparation, 126–27

mission, college and university: choices regarding, 109, 137, 140, 142–43; Great Recession of 2008's effects on, 18; linking with market and management, 2, 6–7, 102; meeting students' needs, 125; values and, 66, 114, 119

MOOCs, 79–82

Moon, Youngme, on need for differentiation, 111–12

motivation, student, 65, 66–67

National Bureau of Economic Research (NBER), recession data from, 151n28

National Employment Law Project, research on unemployment, 56

net worth, family, 15–16, 157n21; Great Recession's effects on, 45, 49, 51, 62–63. *See also* income, family; investment(s): family/personal; savings, personal

Personal Consumption Expenditures, 14, 16–17

Pew Research Center: research on Hispanic students, 38; value survey, 74, 97

prices, college and university: choice affected by, 53, 91–92, 94, 96, 160n8; inflation-adjusted, 3, 60, 61; lack of family savings for, 54, 55; manipulation of, 3–4, 27, 69, 84–85, 93–94, 161n14; reimagining approach to, 132–35; rising, 7, 46–48, 60, 62, 73, 82, 95; sensitivity to, 11, 42–45, 88–94, 99. *See also* income, family: college costs in relation to; tuition; value, of higher education: price's nexus with

private colleges and universities: financial aid picture, 90; prices, 47, 60, 61, 93–94; student loan debt, 58, 59

public colleges and universities: financial aid picture, 90; government appropriations for, 15, 18, 132, 136; increase in numbers of, 9–10; prices, 47, 60, 61, 93–94, 134; student loan debt, 58

public policy, higher education issues, 3, 7; challenges to, 41; changing, 9, 150n8; price control and, 93–94; and reimagining markets, 125, 126; value concerns, 76, 96–99

recruitment, 24, 32–34, 95, 117–21, 126–30. *See also* marketing, by colleges and universities

regulation, federal and state, 4, 93–94, 96–99

return on investment (ROI), higher education, 17, 25, 57, 71–76, 118, 120; gateway to middle class, 10, 40, 45, 56; wage enhancement, 10–11, 14, 48. *See also* investment(s): college degree seen as; value, of higher education: price's nexus with

Revenue Theory of Cost (Bowen), 131–32

risk: in decision making, 2, 19, 119; enrollment, 26, 49, 134; managing, 104, 125; operational, 25, 94

Saint John's University (Minnesota), profile of students, 32, 124

Sallie Mae: on percentage of parent contributions to college expenses, 54; research on perceived value of college education, 71

SAT, test scores, 122, 128, 153n16

savings, personal, 45, 48, 49, 52–55, 61, 62–63. *See also* income, family; investment(s), family/personal; net worth, family

Schumpeter, Joseph, on technological change, 78, 159n18

selectivity, principle of, 31, 87, 124, 153n16

simplicity, in higher education, 64–65

spending: college and university, 110, 131–32, 135–40; debt-based, 16, 48, 57–63, 91; family, 16, 48, 131; vs. saving, 52–53

state appropriations. *See* government, federal and state: appropriations from

stock market, 14, 16, 132; Great Recession's effects on, 18, 49, 50

students, college and university: aspirations of, 38, 39, 65, 66–67, 75, 122, 129; characteristics of, 2, 3, 6, 23, 65, 66–67; degree attainment rates, 4, 39, 76; early preparation of, 126–30, 162nn11–12; economic groups of, 44–45; enrollment trends, 8, 9–10, 13, 150n19; expectations of, 6–9, 28, 92, 95, 98–101, 121–24; international, 32–34; racial and ethnic diversity of, 34, 35–37, 154n31; transfer, 27, 153n7; values and attributes of, 65–67, 74–76, 123–24. *See also* admissions marketplace; choices, student; enrollment; high school–to–college participation rates; recruitment; *and individual racial and ethnic student groups*

students, college and university, traditional-age: changing characteristics of, 2–3, 23, 28, 63, 91, 121–25; decline in numbers of, 12–13, 25, 27; enrollment trends of, 15, 24, 41, 151n19; geographic profile of, 28–34; market for, 24; racial and ethnic diversity of, 36–37; recruitment of, 15; unemployment rates for, 73

students, high school: college enrollment trends, 11, 24, 153n17; graduation rates, 3, 12, 23–24, 35–36, 152nn3–4, 154n29; racial and ethnic diversity of, 35–37, 152n1, 154nn28, 31; regional demographic patterns for, 28–30. *See also* high school–to–college participation rates

Survey of Consumer Finances (Federal Reserve Board), 53–54, 55

sustainability, in higher education, 4–5, 25

taxpayers, support of higher education by, 15, 18, 93–94, 98–99, 132, 136. *See also* government, federal and state: appropriations from

technology. *See* disruption(s): technological;
  higher education: online
Trends in Student Aid (College Board), 58
tuition: cuts in, 69, 161n14; as element of colleges'
  total costs, 44–45; net revenue from, 63, 92, 132,
  135–36; rising, 18, 43, 93. *See also* financial aid;
  prices, college and university

unemployment: college graduates' rates lower, 10,
  14, 72–73; during Great Recession of 2008, 18,
  45, 48, 51, 55–57, 61. *See also* employment,
  college education's enhancement of
universities. *See* colleges and universities; higher
  education
US Department of Education, financial aid data
  from, 90
US News and World Report, college rankings,
  69–70, 78

value, of higher education: challenges to, 4, 48;
  changing, 1–2, 3; creating, 5, 113, 114–15, 119–21;
  decision making based on, 108–21, 143;

economic, 4, 7, 11; expectations of, 2, 84, 92, 96,
  121–24, 130; historic, 64; learning, 72, 74–76; of
  online offerings, 77–80, 82; perceptions of, 9,
  39–40, 42–43, 45, 56–57, 156n6, 159n6, 161n15;
  price's nexus with, 84–85, 87–88, 91–92, 97, 99,
  102, 106, 133–35. *See also* return on investment
  (ROI), higher education
values: collegiate, 3, 66–67, 76, 103; disruption of,
  1, 21, 64–82, 83, 84, 137–39; family, 72–76;
  119–20; student, 65–67, 74–76, 123–24

wages, college degree's enhancement of, 10–11, 14,
  48. *See also* income, family
wealth: accumulated, 50, 131–32, 157n21; creation
  of, 13, 16. *See also* net worth, family
Western Interstate Commission for Higher
  Education (WICHE), projections of high
  school graduates, 23, 35–36, 154n29
white student population, 35, 37, 39–41
willingness to pay, 7, 92. *See also* ability
  to pay
women, college enrollment by, 9, 10, 13, 151n19